チャペックの本棚
ヨゼフ・チャペックの装丁デザイン

Čapek's Bookshelf
The Book Design of Josef Čapek

千野栄一さんに捧ぐ
For Prof. Eiichi Chino

目次 / Contents

ヨゼフ・チャペックの表紙 / 千野栄一 ……………………… 7
Josef Čapek's Book Jackets / Eiichi Chino

本の表紙 / ヨゼフ・チャペック ……………………………… 107
Book Covers / Josef Čapek

本の表紙はどのように作るか / ヨゼフ・チャペック ……… 115
How to make Book Jackets / Josef Čapek

作品リスト / List of Works ………………………………… 191

ヨゼフ・チャペックの表紙
千野栄一

1

　1958年の11月、第二次世界大戦後の第1回の交換留学生としてチェコのプラハに到着したとき、ヨゼフについての私の知識というものは限りなくゼロに近いものであった。間違いなく知っていたことはカレル・チャペックの兄で画家、それも挿絵画家でカレルの『長い長いお医者さんの話』※1の挿絵を描いたというくらいである。出発の前から本は好きで、プラハへ着いたら古本屋回りをしようと思っていたし、最初に泊められたヴァーツラフ広場に面したホテルの近くに新本屋に混じって古本屋もあって、翌日からそれらを巡り歩いてチャペックの本をすぐ揃えようという希望で最初の晩の眠りに就いた。
　そのあと数日は学生寮に入る手続きやら、いろいろな事務手続きがあって、やっと古本屋にいってみると、どうやら日本とは違うことに気づかされた。古本屋の店頭は賑やかだが、中に入ってみるとガランとしていることが多く、客が本を選ぶというよりは本があるかないかお伺いをたて、もしあれば売っていただくという雰囲気である。
　よく観察してみると、チャペックの本でいつでも手に入るのは『第1救援隊』※2と『母』※3だけであることが分かった。前者は落盤事故における炭鉱労働者の連帯を描き、後者はスペイン市民戦争への反フランコ闘争を描いているからというのである。この頃の社会主義リアリズムの単細胞的な単純明快さときたら、水戸黄門か西部劇である。その他のチャペックの本はほぼ発禁書扱いで、それをきいても「たまたま今は持ち合わせがありません」と、まるでマニュアルにでもあるかのように、どこでも同じ返事が戻ってきた。『絶対子工場』※4も、『経外典』※5も、『マルシアス、あるいは文学の周辺』※6もそうであった。これが社会主義下の古本屋であった。
　そんな訳で、1920〜1930年代のチャペックの古本などお目にかかったことなどなかった。古本屋は木曜の夜、閉店してからウィンドウを飾り、そこに時々チャペックの本が出ていた。そこで金曜日の朝一番で並んで、もし自分の前までに売れなければ買うの

である。2冊いい本があっても同時に2冊は買えず、もう一度行列の後ろにつくのであるから、入手できる可能性はほとんどない。

1920～1930年代のチャペックの古本が手に入るようになったのは、チャペックについての本『ポケットのなかのチャペック』(晶文社)※7を書いて、古本屋でチャペック研究者と認められるようになってからである。これが出版されたのは1975年であるので、何とチャペックの本を探し始めてからもう17年の歳月がたっていた。

この頃にはもう主な古本屋とは知り合いになり、珍しいものが出ると取って置いてくれることもあったが、何はともあれ定期的に回ることが肝要であった。古本屋の中で、ユングマン通りにあった買入れ専門店のミロスラフ・ジグムントさん、文化財輸出入公団アルティアの古書輸出部長マンジェル博士、親子2代に世話になったフラーフさん父子の4人が私のコレクションの源泉である。『ヨゼフ・チャペックと本』※8なるヨゼフの表紙を集めた本が、私がチェコに初めて足を踏み入れた年に立派に出版されているのであるから、もしそのことを知っていたら、ポツポツにしても買い集めなかったかもしれない。このヴラジミール・ティーレの本すら入手できたのは十数年後のことなので、無知というものは強いものである。ティーレはいかにしてヨゼフの表紙の本を集めたかを小説以上におもしろく書いているので、そちらを読んでいただきたい。

要するに私のコレクションは気がついたら集まっていたという訳で、散文的なことこのうえない。ただ40年は蒐集(しゅうしゅう)を続けたことになる。もう1つ、近年になって数冊やや高いお金を出して買ったもの以外は、本当にタバコ代と同じ費用の本であったことも自慢である。

昨年から話が持ち上がって、私の勤務する和光大学の図書館の一角を利用して2週間の展示※9が計画され、近く実現されるので、もし成功すればその他の機関でも同じ展示が計画される可能性がある。

2

「ヨゼフの表紙」といわれても、それを見たことがない人は何を想像するであろうか？そのような人々にこのタイトルで何を伝えたらいいのであろうか。「ヨゼフの表紙」とは主として1920年から1930年にかけて、再利用した表紙約150点をも含めた500点のヨゼフがデザインした表紙の総称である。本来自分は画家だと思っていたヨゼフが、偶然の巡り合わせでグラフィック・デザインに手を染め、好評であったがためにこれだけの仕事をしたもので

ある。

　当時、1920年代の初頭の本はフランスの本で今でもよく見られるように、その本の題名だけが書かれていただけであった（フランスの名誉のために一言すれば、もし読んだあと蔵書として残すのであればその家に伝わっているその家の装丁の革綴じにし、そうでなければそのまま捨てるという厳しい選択が待っている訳である）。

　そこへ本の内容とつながっていく、表紙を描こうというのである。この時代はキュービズムから始まって、アール・ヌーボー、アール・デコと続き、ダダイズムからシュールレアリズムが起こった時代である。

　ただ表紙の芸術というのにはいろいろな制約があって、芸術家にとっては決して嬉しくない舞台である。芸術を表現する素材として、彫刻なら、木、石、金属があり、絵画では、カンバス、紙、壁、天井などがあって、そこに十分に自分の芸術が展開できる。ところが本の表紙は場所として大きく制限される。さらに機能面で本の内容への導入という役割で縛られることになる。

　ヨゼフ・チャペックも最初のうち、自分は画家でグラフィック・デザイナーではないと明白に告白している。なぜそのような仕事を引き受けたのかという問いに、チェコの詩人ヤン・ネルダの詩で、Vším jsem byl rád.（何であっても私は嬉しい）と答えているが、この世にいて、何であろうとも、それであったことそのものに喜びがあったと言っている。すなわち偶然にせよ回ってきた仕事に全力を尽くすという仕事への倫理観があり、それに若干のお金もと小さい声で加えているが、ヨゼフはあくまで正直である。

　そして気づいてみたとき、画家で芸術理論家であり、詩人で作家でと十分以上の十二分の活躍の中に、添え物ではなく「表紙の芸術」も業績の一画としてあるのである。

3

　今日、ヨゼフの表紙は見事にまとまったユニークな分野としての地位を確立している。

　チェコでは、さらにこの表紙の分野においてアヴァンギャルド芸術が進出していて、その理論家で作者であったカレル・タイゲを中心にシュテイルスキー、トワィアン、ムルクヴィチカ、ツィリル・ボウダなどのグラフィック・デザイナーの伝統はさらに1940～1950年代へ受け継がれており、サイドルの作品も一目てその伝統の流れにある。さらに現代の表紙を見たときも、粋に垢抜けして、洗練されているデザインにその面影がある。

もう1昨年前だったか、この時期の作品をアメリカの図書館の協力で展示した「第125回　チェコ・アヴァンギャルドブックデザイン1920―'30s展」※10が銀座であり、見ごたえのあるものだったが、英文のカタログだけあってどうしても全体の姿がとらえられないようなもどかしさと、商業主義的な匂いがあって残念な気がした。

　ヨゼフ自身で表紙を作り始めたときは、第1次世界大戦後で彫る材料がなくリノリウムに彫ることになり、逆に素朴な味わいを出している。しかし、リノリウムは多量の枚数を刷るのに耐えられないので、本がよく売れて2,000部を過ぎると、ヨゼフはもう一度同じものを彫ったのである。ヨゼフの真面目さというか、表紙のコレクションとしては数が増えることになった。

　ヨゼフの表紙について語るときは、いつもことばというものの限界を感じ、「百聞は一見にしかず」という格言の重さを味わう。特に作品が500と限られていれば、その作品の分析もほぼ終わっており、シュールレアリズム的なもの、フォークロアの要求の強いもの、面を基本にしたもの、記号的なもの、絵画的なもの、作品の文中に踏み込んだものと分類され、それが統合的だといわれ、作品を見ながらそれに同意しながらうなずくことができる。

　1つ1つが丁寧になされ、毎回ポイントのある表紙がこのように作り出されるヨゼフの才能にはチェコ語でいうklobouk dolů（クロボウク・ドルー）、「帽子を軽くとって、敬意の挨拶をする」以外の何物も私は知らない。

※1 童話集。1932年刊行。
　　原題 'Devatero pohádek a ještě jedna od Josefa Čapka jako přívažek「九つのお話ともう一つヨゼフ・チャペックのおまけのお話」'。『長い長いお医者さんの話』は、邦訳でのタイトル。
※2 小説。1937年刊行。原題 'První parta'。
※3 戯曲。1938年刊行。原題 'Matka'。
※4 小説。1922年刊行。原題 'Továrna na absolutno'。邦訳『絶対子工場』。
※5 短篇集。1945年刊行。原題 'Kniha apokryfů'。邦訳『経外典』。
※6 文芸評論集。1931年刊行。原題 'Marsyas čili na okraj literatury'。
※7 本書の著者による著作。3年間にわたるチャペックおよびその著作についての雑誌・新聞等への連載をまとめたもの。
※8 原題 'Josef Čapek a kniha'。
※9 2000年5月13日〜5月26日まで和光大学図書館梅根記念館で開催された「チェコ アバンギャルド ブックデザイン展」のこと。
※10 1996年10月4日から10月26日まで銀座のDNPギャラリーで開催された。アメリカのファーレイ・ディッキンソン大学図書館エマ・ダナ・コレクション所蔵によるヨゼフ・チャペック、カレル・タイゲなどのブックデザイン120点が展示された。

Josef Čapek's Book Jackets
Eiichi Chino

1

When I arrived in Prague in November 1958 with the first group of exchange students after World War II, I knew next to nothing about Josef Čapek. What I did know was that he was the older brother of the writer Karel Čapek, and that he was a painter and an illustrator who had provided the illustrations for Karel's 'The Long, Long Doctor's Story'#1. I had always loved books, and it was my intention on arriving in Prague to visit all the secondhand bookstores. We were initially put up at a hotel on Wenceslas Square, and there were plenty of bookstores nearby, some of them sellers of old books. I went to bed the first night hoping to start the very next day visiting these stores with a view to building up a collection of Čapek books.

For the next few days, however, I was kept busy with arrangements for moving into a student dormitory and other procedural matters, and when I finally got to visit the bookstores, I discovered that in some respects they were very different from bookstores in Japan. Plenty of people clustered around the shop fronts, but inside they were usually entirely empty. Customers didn't seem to browse, looking for books to buy; they came to inquire if the store had a particular book, and if it had, they asked if they might be permitted to buy it.

I noticed that the only Čapek books you could obtain almost everywhere were 'The First Rescue Party'#2 and 'The Mother'#3. Perhaps this was because the former is about solidarity among coal miners at the time of a mine cave-in, and the latter describes the anti-Franco protests that led to the Spanish Civil War. The 'socialist realism' of those times brought a mindless, simplistic, black-or-white approach to everything. Other Čapek books were mostly treated as banned, and if you asked for one of them you always got exactly the same answer, almost as though it had been deliberately memorized: 'I'm afraid we don't happen to have it at the moment'. This applied to such famous works as 'The Absolute at Large'#4, 'Apocryphal Tales'#5 and 'Marsyas'#6.

This was how secondhand booksellers operated under the socialist regime. As a result, I never got to see any old Čapek editions from the twenties and thirties. After the stores closed on Thursday nights they would change their window displays and occasionally a Čapek book would appear. So on the Friday morning I'd be one of the first in line, and if the book hadn't already been sold I would buy it. On occasion there were two books worth having, but we couldn't buy two at once, so I would have to go to the back of the line again, which meant the chances of getting the second book were almost nil.

I didn't obtain any twenties or thirties Čapek editions until I myself produced a book on Čapek called 'Poketto no naka no Čapek'#7 (Čapek in my Pocket) published by Shobunsha, and was accepted at the bookstores as a Čapek scholar. But my book was published only in 1975, and by then 17 long years had passed since the start of my search.

By that time, however, I was on friendly terms with the proprietors of the leading stores, and when something unusual turned up they would put it aside for me, so it was imperative to visit them regularly. Four people supplied most of my collection: Miloslav Zikmund, a specialist purchaser on Jungmann Street, a Doctor Manzel, manager of the antiquarian book export department of Artia, a public corporation handling trade in cultural assets, and two generations, father and son, of the Hrach family. In fact, a fine book incorporating a collection of Čapek jackets, called 'Josef Čapek and his Books'#8 had been published the year I first set foot in the country, and if I had known of it I may not have spent so many years collecting the books individually. But I didn't obtain even this book, compiled by Vladimir Thiele, until 10 or more years later. Thiele's story of how he came to collect the books makes fascinating reading and I would strongly recommend it.

Thus my own collection grew little by little, with nothing planned or systematic about it. But I went on collecting for 40 years. I also like to boast that, apart from a few recent purchases for which I paid quite a lot, these books cost me hardly more than a pack of cigarettes.

Discussions began last year on holding a two-week exhibition of Čapek's book jackets#9 in the library at Wako University, where I work, and this is shortly due to take place. If it does well it may be possible to arrange for the exhibit to be shown at other institutions.

2

How can people who have never seen Josef Čapek's book jackets imagine what they are like? What should I say about them? I'm referring to the 500 books with jackets designed by Josef Čapek that were published mostly during the 1920s and

30s, including some 150 jackets of recycled designs. Josef thought of himself as a painter, but chance circumstances caused him to try his hand in graphic design, and it was because these efforts were well received that he produced such a large body of work in this field.

At the start of the 1920s he worked on French books which then, as now very often, had only the title on the cover. (By way of explanation, this was in part because books were subject to a harsh choice. If the owner decided to keep the book after reading it, it would be bound in leather. Otherwise the book would be immediately discarded.)

So Čapek sought to design jackets that related to the content of the book. This was the period that started with cubism, to be followed by art nouveau and art deco, and then dadaism and surrealism.

There are a number of limitations imposed on book jacket design, and as a medium it is far from ideal for the artist. A sculptor can work with wood, stone or metal, and for painting there is canvas and paper, or walls and ceilings. All these give the artist plenty of scope to express his artistry. But book jackets are severely restricted size-wise, and they must also serve a function, the jacket's role being to introduce the content of the book.

From the beginning Josef Čapek made it very clear that he was a painter, not a graphic designer. When asked why he accepted commissions for this sort of work, he answered with a line from the Czech poet Jan Neruda 'Vším jsem byl rád.' (Whatever I do, I am happy). He meant that wherever he was in this world, whatever he did, he could find pleasure in it. In other words, he had a strong ethical sense in that, whatever sort of job happened to come his way he would do his very best. And he would add sotto voce that he'd also be glad to receive a little money. Josef was nothing if not honest.

But in truth, among all the many activities he took on —many more than most— as a painter, an art theoretician, a poet and a writer, his book jacket design was no mere sideline, but represented a substantial portfolio of achievement.

3

Josef's book jackets have today an established position as a genre in their own right.

What followed in this field was avant-garde art, and a tradition of graphic designers, starting with the theoretician and artist Karel Teige, and including Styrsky, Toyen, Mrkvicka, and Cyril Bouda, continued through the 40s and 50s. A glance at Seydl's work shows that it is also part of that tradition. Even contemporary book jackets hark back to it in their chic elegance, in the refinement of their design.

A year or two ago, an exhibit arranged by an American library entitled 'Czech Avant-garde Book Design, 1920s and 30s'#10 came to Ginza in Tokyo. It was well worth seeing, but I was irritated that the catalogue was only in English, making it difficult to get a complete understanding, and disappointed at the commercialized presentation.

Josef himself began his work just after World War I when there were few proper materials available, so he cut out his designs in linoleum, which had the effect of emphasizing their lack of sophistication. Linoleum, though, is not very durable, and if more than 2,000 copies were printed he would make a new lino cut of the same design. This testifies to Josef's diligence, but it also served to increase the numbers of jackets for collectors.

Talking about Josef's book jackets I feel the limitations of language, and realize how true it is that 'there's nothing quite like seeing for oneself'. Restricted to 500 main works, a classification is almost complete. It includes surrealistic works, those drawing on folklore, abstract designs to fit the front cover, those using signs and symbols, pictorial designs, and those based on the content of the text. If it's said to be comprehensive, I can look at his work and bow my head in agreement.

For Josef's prodigious talent, demonstrated in the attentive way he produced every jacket, with each one making its own particular point, I know no better way to express my feeling than with the Czech expression 'klobouk dolů', which means to lightly doff one's hat in profound respect.

#1 Collection of stories for children, published in 1932. Czech title: Devatero pohádek a ještě jedna od Josefa Čapka jako přívažek (Nine Fairy Tales and One More Thrown In For Good Measure). 'The Long, Long Doctor's Story' is the English equivalent of the title of the Japanese translation.
#2 Novel published in 1937. Czech title: První parta
#3 Playscript published in 1938. Czech title: Matka
#4 Novel published in 1922. Czech title: Továrna na absolutno
#5 Short story collection published in 1932. Czech title: Kniha apokryfů
#6 Literary criticism, published in 1931. Czech title: 'Marsyas' čili na okraj literatury
#7 The author compiled the material for this book from newspaper and magazine articles he contributed on Čapek and his work over a period of three years.
#8 Czech title: Josef Čapek a kniha.
#9 This exhibition was called 'Czech Avant-garde Book Design' and was held in the Wako University Library Umene Memorial Hall from 13 to 26 May, 2000.
#10 This exhibit, held at the DNP Gallery, Ginza, from 4 to 26 October, 1996, featured 120 jacket designs of Josef Čapek, Karel Teige and others, from a collection held at Fairleigh Dickinson University.

Nejskromnější umění / Josef Čapek
The Most Modest Art / Josef Čapek
最も謙虚な芸術 / ヨゼフ・チャペック
1st ed. / 初版
1920

Francouzská poesie nové doby / Karel Čapek
New Era French Poetry / Karel Čapek
新時代のフランス詩 / カレル・チャペック
1st ed. / 初版
1920

19

20

Kritika slov / Karel Čapek
A Critique of Words / Karel Čapek
言葉の批評 / カレル・チャペック
1st ed. / 初版
1920

Kritika slov / Karel Čapek
A Critique of Words / Karel Čapek
言葉の批評 / カレル・チャペック
2nd ed. / 2版
1927

Loupežník

Three-act comedy. A professor has two daughters.
After the elder elopes with her lover, the parents are concerned about the younger.
Enter a young man, the 'robber' of the title, who steals the younger daughter's heart.
The professor seeks help from various quarters, but in vain.
However, when the elder daughter, now deserted by her lover,
comes home with her child, the young man abandons his love and departs.

3幕の戯曲（喜劇）。教授には2人の娘、ロラとミミがいた。
ロラは恋人と家を出てしまったため両親はミミを失うのを恐れている。
そこに「盗人」である若者がやってきてミミの心を奪ってしまう。
教授はいろいろな人に助けを求めるが無駄に終わる。
そのとき男に捨てられた姉のロラが子供を連れて戻ってくる。
それを見た若者はひとりで家を去って行く。

24

 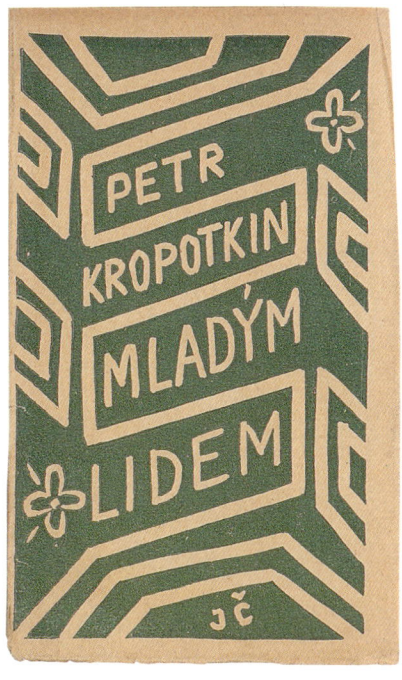

Loupežník / Karel Čapek
The Robber / Karel Čapek
盗人 / カレル・チャペック
1st ed. / 1版
1920

Mladým lidem / Petr Kropotkin
An Appeal to the Young / Petr Kropotkin
若い人々へ / ピョートル・クロポトキン
1st ed. / 初版
1920

Malé děvče / Helena Čapková
The Small Girl / Helena Čapková
小さな少女 / ヘレナ・チャプコヴァー
1st ed. / 初版
1920

26

R. U. R.

Three-act play that coined the term 'robot'.
Set to do the work of human beings,
mechanical slaves called robots grow upset
and rise up against their human masters.
They attempt to supplant human beings and discover the secrets of life.

3幕の戯曲。人造人間にロボットという名前が初めてつけられた作品。
人間の労働を肩代わりしていた機械のロボットたちが感情を持ち、
人間に対して反乱をおこす。ロボットは人間にとってかわろうとして
生命の秘密をさぐろうとする。

KAREL ČAPEK

R.U.R.

ROBOTS

UNIVERSAL

ROSSUM'S

DRAMA

R.U.R. (Rossum's Universal Robots) / Karel Čapek
R.U.R. (Rossum's Universal Robots) / Karel Čapek
R.U.R.（ロッスムのユニバーサルロボット）/ カレル・チャペック
1st ed. / 初版
1920

R.U.R. (Rossum's Universal Robots) / Karel Čapek
R.U.R. (Rossum's Universal Robots) / Karel Čapek
R.U.R.（ロッスムのユニバーサルロボット）/ カレル・チャペック
2nd ed. / 2版
1921

R.U.R. (Rossum's Universal Robots) / Karel Čapek
R.U.R. (Rossum's Universal Robots) / Karel Čapek
R.U.R.（ロッスムのユニバーサルロボット）/ カレル・チャペック
4th ed. / 4版
1922

R.U.R. (Rossum's Universal Robots) / Karel Čapek
R.U.R. (Rossum's Universal Robots) / Karel Čapek
R.U.R.（ロッスムのユニバーサルロボット）/ カレル・チャペック
6th ed. / 6版
1924

31

32

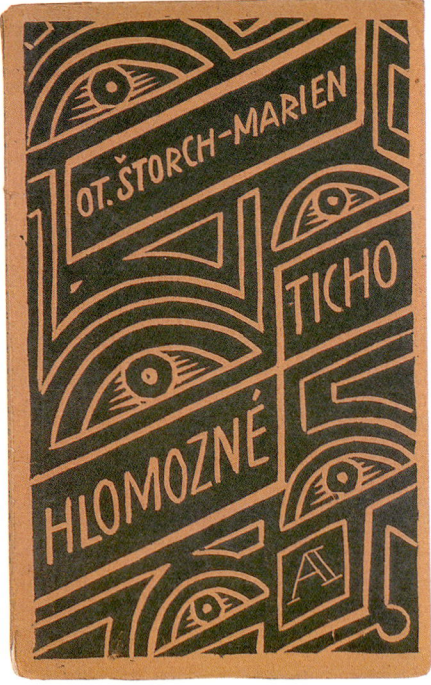

Povídky z městského sadu / Marie Pujmanová - Hennerová
Tales from the City Orchard / Marie Pujmanová - Hennerová
市街地の果樹園の物語 / マリエ・プイノヴァー - ヘネロヴァー
1st ed. / 初版
1920

Hlomozné ticho / Otakar Štorch - Marien
Noisy Silence / Otakar Štorch - Marien
騒がしい静寂 / オタカル・シュトルフ - マリエン
1st ed. / 初版
1920

Mistr Petr Pleticha / anonymus
Master Peter Patelin / Author unknown
マスター・ペトル・プレチハ（ピエール・パトラン）/ 作者不詳
1st ed. / 初版
1921

34

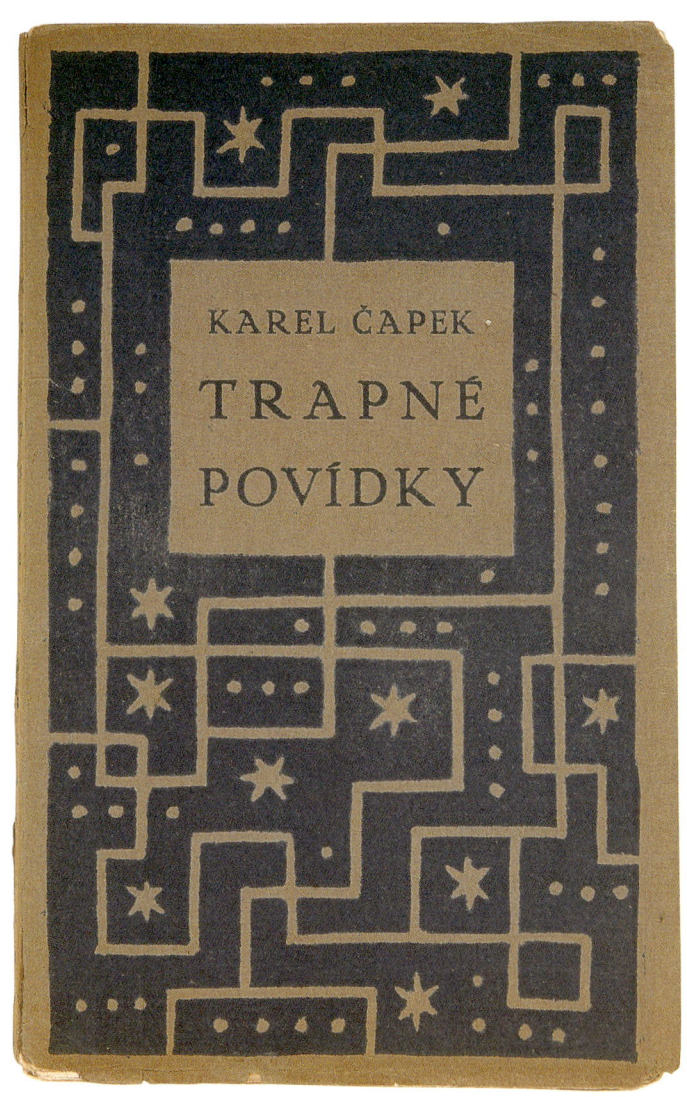

Trapné povídky / Karel Čapek
Embarrassing Short Stories / Karel Čapek
苦悩に満ちた物語 / カレル・チャペック
1st ed. / 初版
1921

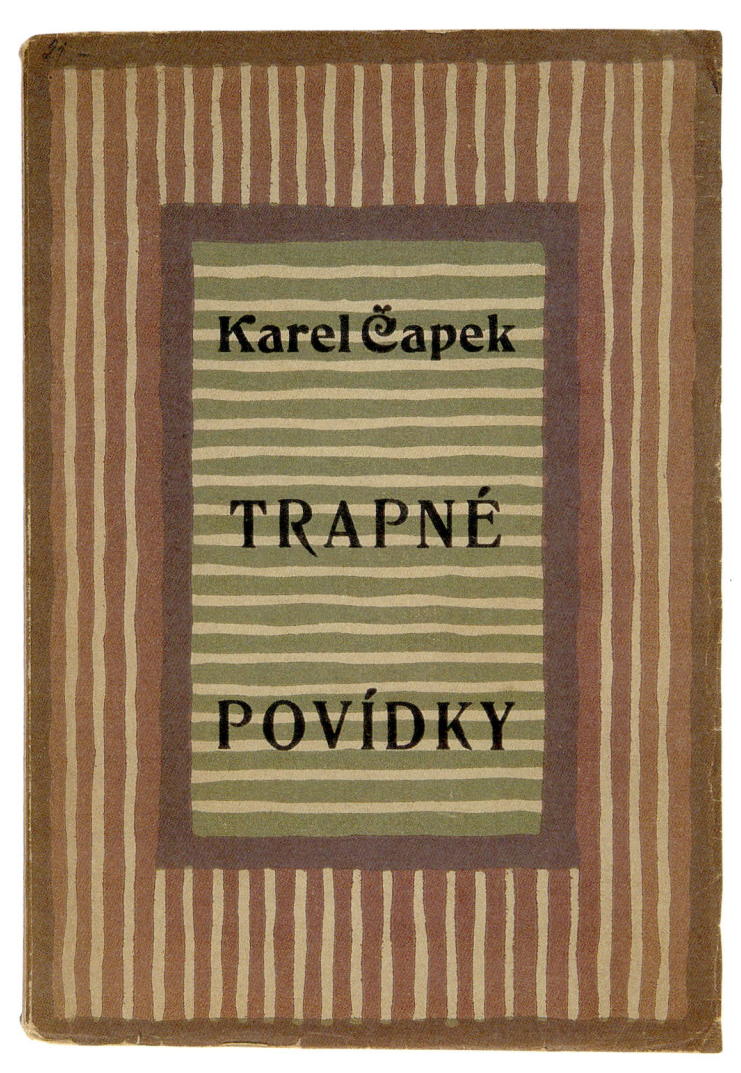

35

Trapné povídky / Karel Čapek
Embarrassing Short Stories / Karel Čapek
苦悩に満ちた物語 / カレル・チャペック
2nd ed. / 2版
1926

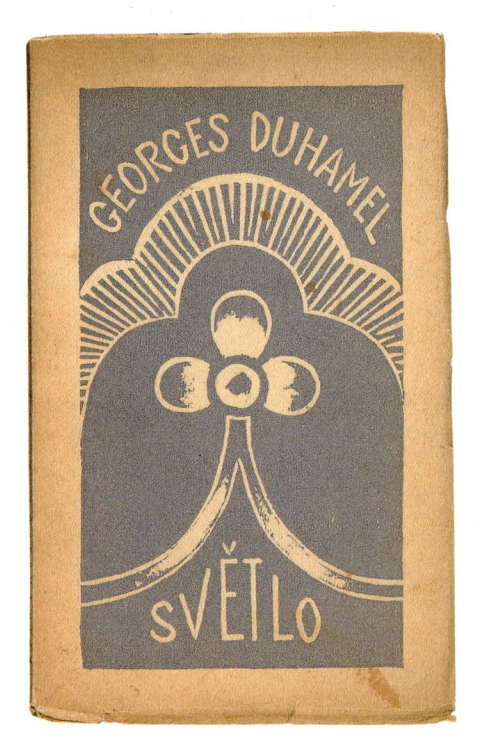

Světlo / Georges Duhamel
Light / Georges Duhamel
光 / ジョルジュ・デュアメル
1st ed. / 初版
1921

Pokušení svatého Antonína / Gustav Flaubert
The Temptation of Saint Anthony / Gustav Flaubert
聖アントワーヌの誘惑 / ギュスターヴ・フロベール
1st ed. / 初版
1921

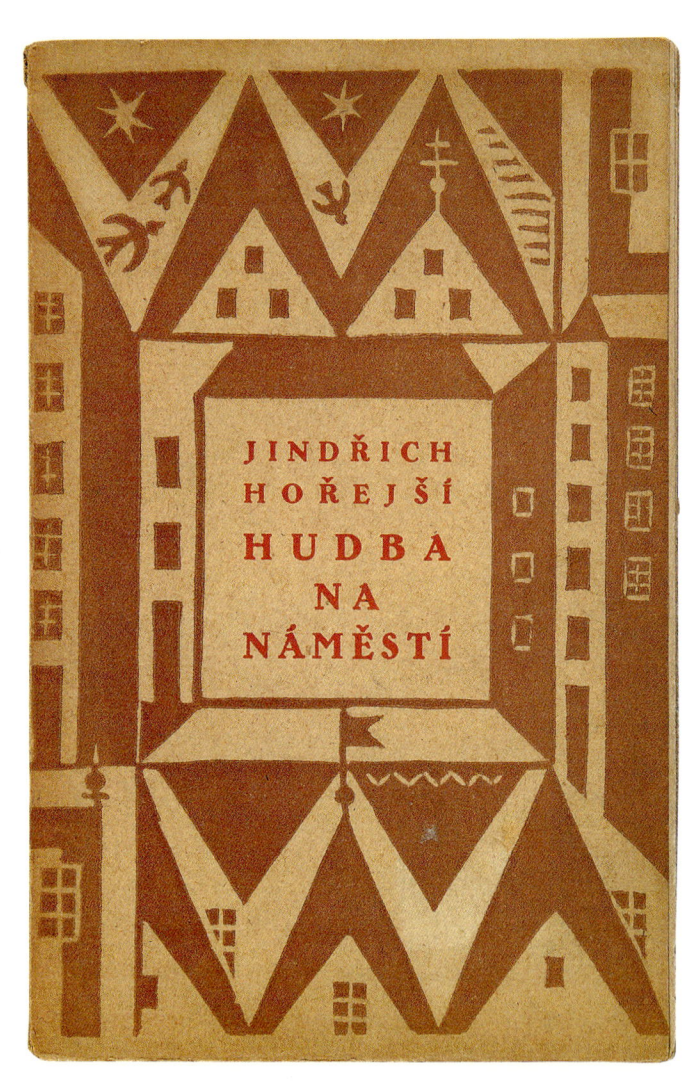

Hudba na náměstí / Jindřich Hořejši
Music in the Square / Jindřich Hořejši
広場の音楽 / インドジフ・ホジェイシー
1st ed. / 初版
1921

39

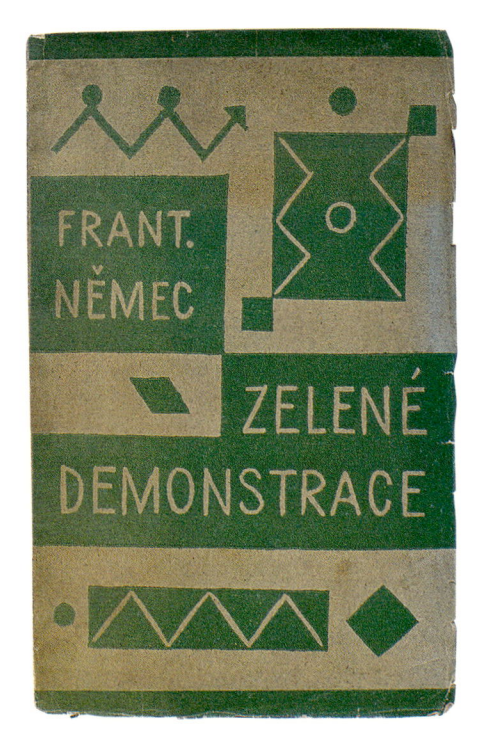

20

Zelené demonstrace / František Němec
Demonstration / František Němec
緑色の表明 / フランチシェク・ニェメツ
1st ed. / 初版
1921

Sen o zástupu zoufajících / Stanislav Kostka Neumann
Dreams of Despairing People / Stanislav Kostka Neumann
絶望する人々についての夢 / スタニスラフ・コストカ・ノイマン
1st ed. / 初版
1921

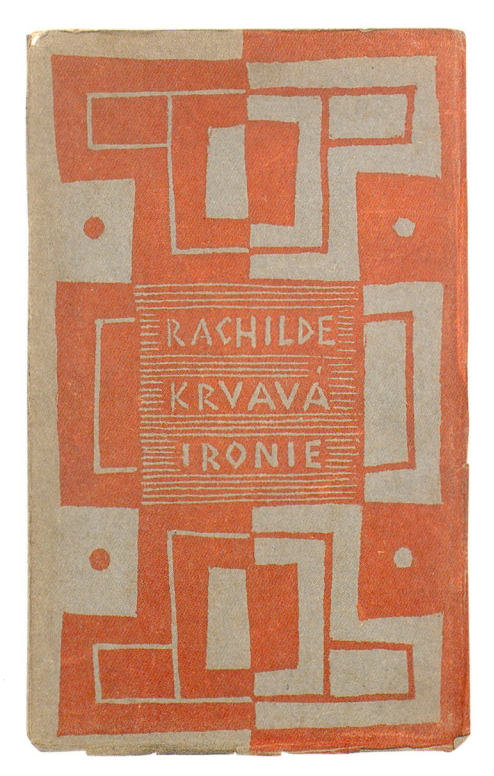

Krvavá ironie / Rachilde
Blood Irony / Rachilde
血に染まった皮肉 / ラシルド
1st ed. / 初版
1921

42

Věc Makropulos

Play in three acts and one scene.
During a court case on a 97-year-old inheritance dispute,
a 'young' woman 300 years old is conjured up by secret means,
and gives testimony on events 100 years earlier.

3幕と1場の戯曲
97年続いた相続問題の裁判中に、
秘法によって300歳でありながら若々しさをたもっている女性が現われ、
100年前のことについて証言することによっていろいろな問題が起こる。

DIVADELNÍ HRY KARLA ČAPKA

KAREL ČAPEK

VĚC

MAKROPULOS

SVAZEK III. / III. VYDÁNÍ / AVENTINUM PRAHA

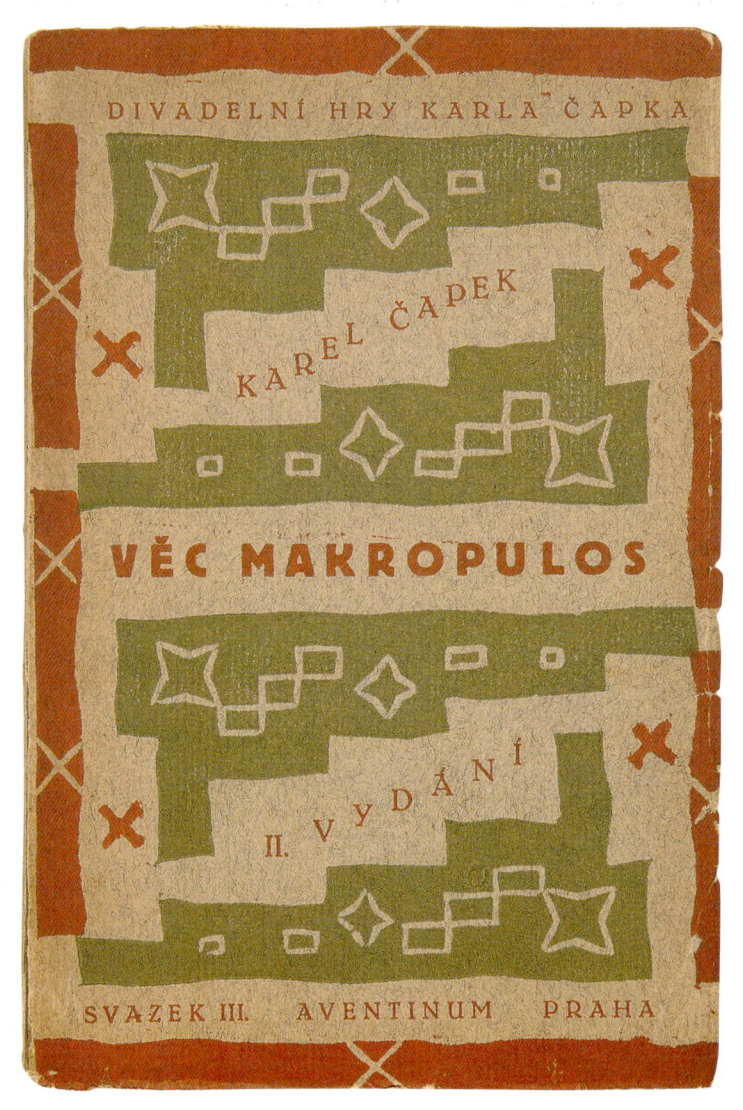

Věc Makropulos / Karel Čapek
The Makropulos Secret / Karel Čapek
マクロプロス事件 / カレル・チャペック
2nd ed. / 2版
1922

45

DIVADELNÍ HRY KARLA ČAPKA

KAREL ČAPEK

VĚC

MAKROPULOS

SVAZEK III. / III. VYDÁNÍ / AVENTINUM PRAHA

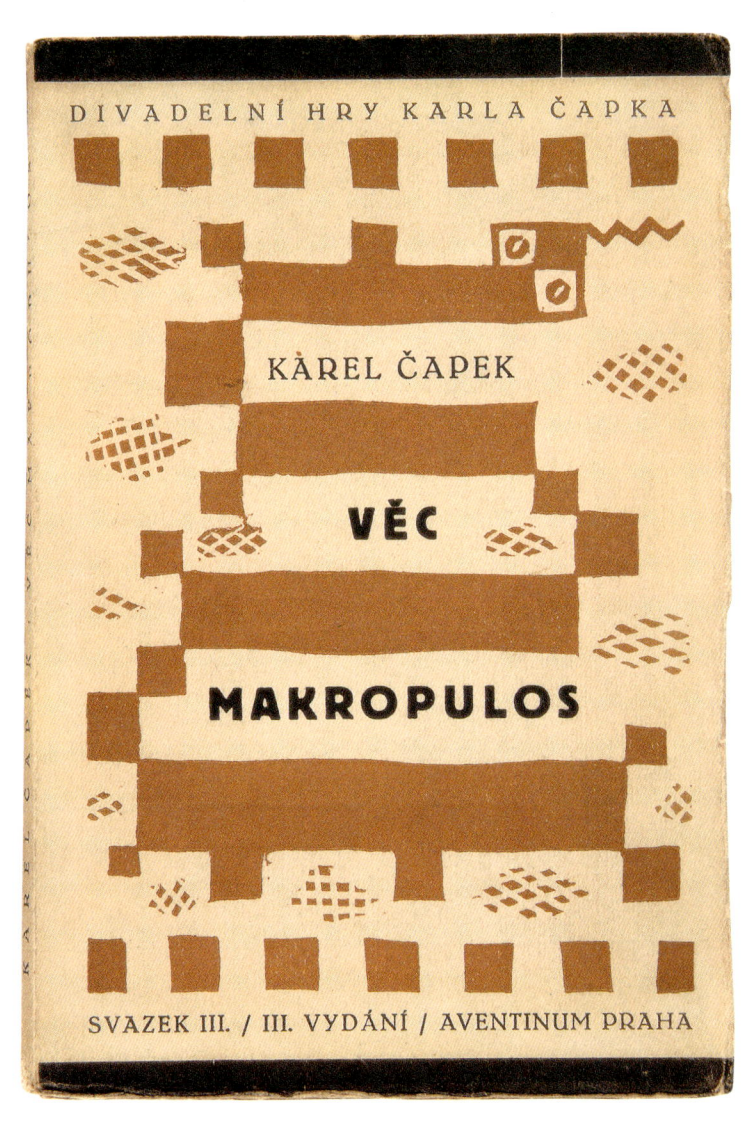

Věc Makropulos / Karel Čapek
The Makropulos Secret / Karel Čapek
マクロプロス事件 / カレル・チャペック
3rd ed. / 3版
1923

Kolébka / Helena Čapková
Cradle / Helena Čapková
揺りかご / ヘレナ・チャプコヴァー
1st ed. / 初版
1922

47

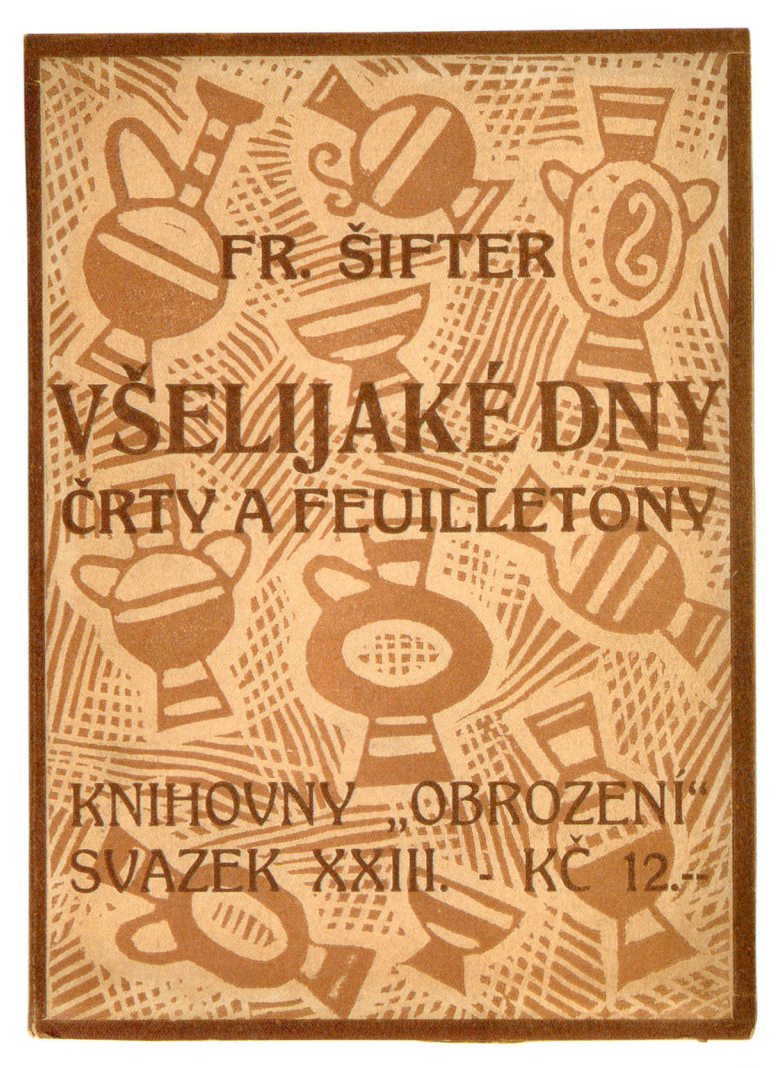

Všelijaké dny / František Šifter
All Sorts of Days / František Šifter
あらゆる日々 / フランチシェク・シフテル
1st ed. / 初版
1922

49

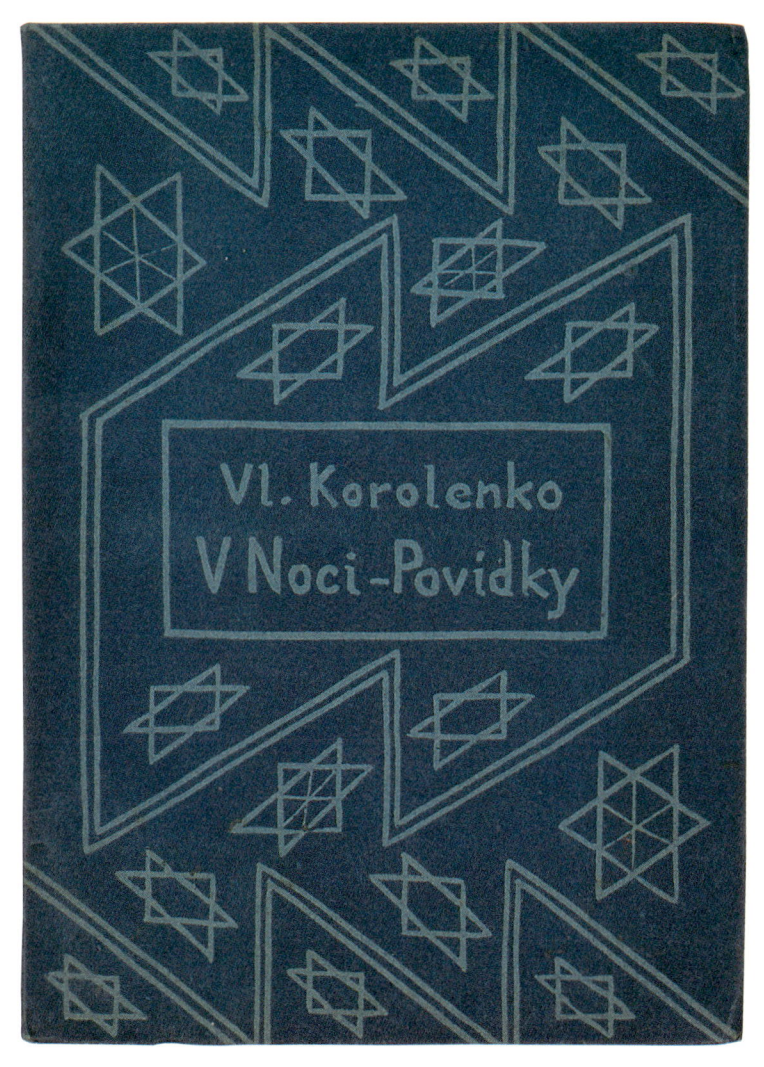

V noci / Vladimir Korolenko
At Night / Vladimir Korolenko
夜に / ウラジーミル・コロレンコ
1st ed. / 初版
1922

Ze života hmyzu

A three-act play satirizing aspects of human life through the life of insects.
The first act uses the habits of a butterfly to portray falling in love,
the second is concerned with human self-centredness,
and the third act projects state egotism through the lives of ants.

虫の生活を通して人間生活を風刺した3幕の戯曲。
第1幕では蝶の生活を描きつつ恋について、
第2幕では人間の利己主義について、
第3幕ではアリの生活に国家的エゴイズムを投影している。

BRATŘÍ ČAPKOVÉ
KOMEDIE

ZE ŽIVOTA HMYZU
II. VYDÁNÍ

52

Ze života hmyzu / Bratří Čapkové
The Life of the Insects / Josef & Karel Čapek
虫の生活 / チャペック兄弟
3rd ed. / 3版
1922

Ze života hmyzu / Bratří Čapkové
The Life of the Insects / Josef & Karel Čapek
虫の生活 / チャペック兄弟
2nd ed. / 2版
1922

54

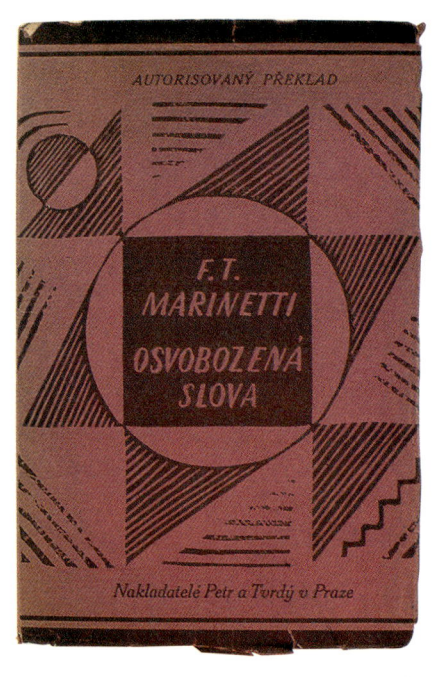

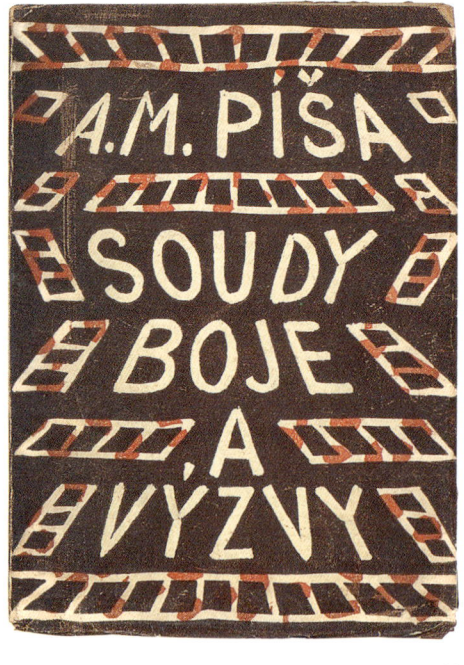

Osvobozená slova / F. T. Marinetti
Manifesto of Futurism / F. T. Marinetti
解放された言葉 / F. T. マリネッティ
2nd ed. / 2版
1922

Soudy, boje a výzvy let 1920-22 / A. M. Píša
Judgements, Struggles and Appeals of the Years 1920-22 / A. M. Píša
1920-22年の判決、戦い、そして訴え / A. M. ピーシャ
1st ed. / 初版
1922

Lásky hra osudná / Bratři Čapkové
Love's Fateful Game / Josef & Karel Čapek
愛の運命のいたずら / チャペック兄弟
1st ed. / 初版
1922

56

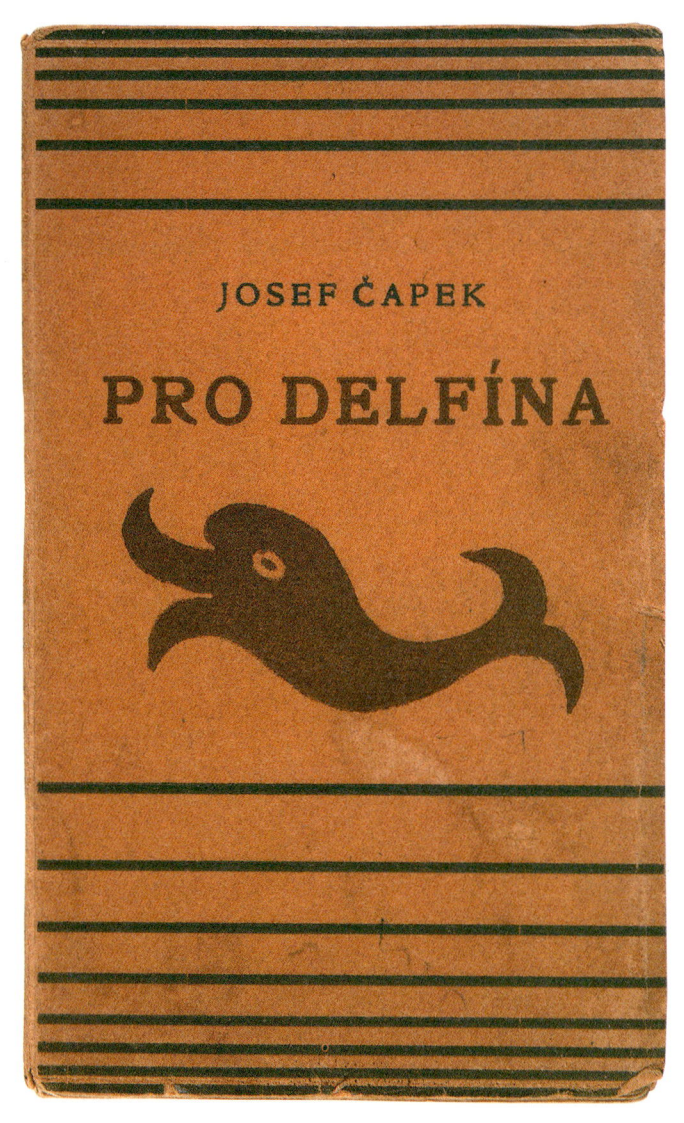

Pro delfína / Josef Čapek
For the Dolphin / Josef Čapek
イルカのために / ヨゼフ・チャペック
1st ed. / 初版
1923

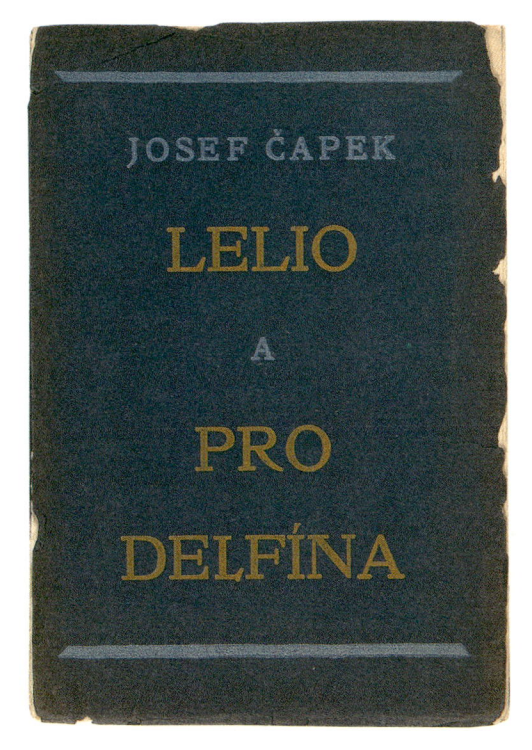

57

Lelio a Pro delfína / Josef Čapek
Lelio & For the Dolphin / Josef Čapek
レーリオとイルカのために / ヨゼフ・チャペック
2nd ed. / 2版
1925

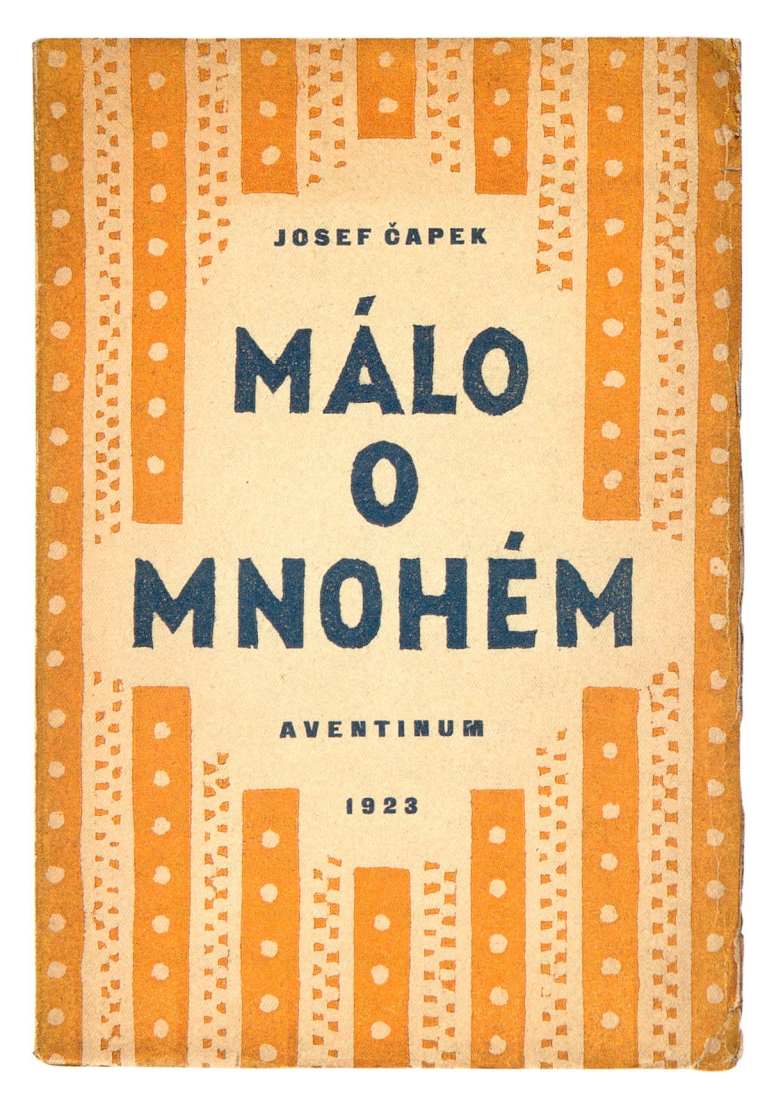

Málo o mnohém / Josef Čapek
A Little about a Lot of Things / Josef Čapek
たくさんのことについて少し / ヨゼフ・チャペック
1st ed. / 初版
1923

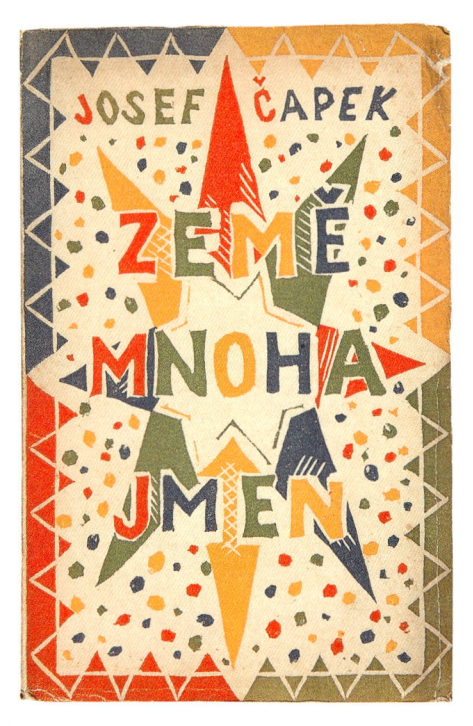

36

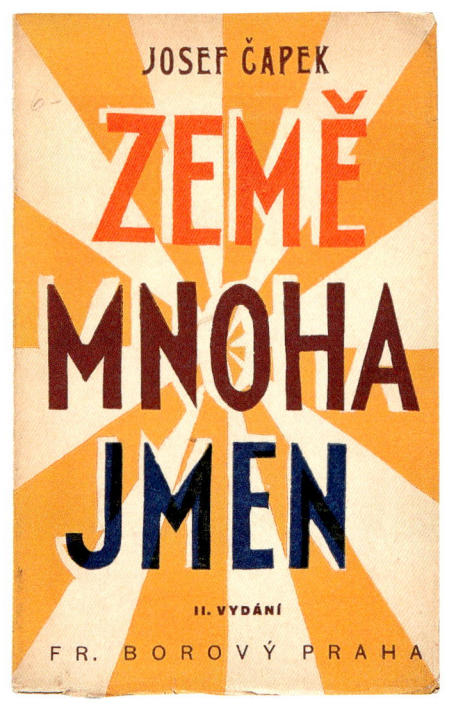

37

Země mnoha jmen / Josef Čapek
The Country with Many Names / Josef Čapek
たくさんの名前を持つ国 / ヨゼフ・チャペック
1st ed. / 初版
1923

Země mnoha jmen / Josef Čapek
The Country with Many Names / Josef Čapek
たくさんの名前を持つ国 / ヨゼフ・チャペック
2nd ed. / 2版
1923

60

Italské listy

Karel Čapek's memoirs of visits to Rome, Palermo, Tuscany, etc.

カレル・チャペックのイタリア旅行記
ローマ、パレルモ、トスカーナなどを巡った

KAREL ČAPEK
ITALSKÉ LISTY

TŘETÍ VYDÁNÍ

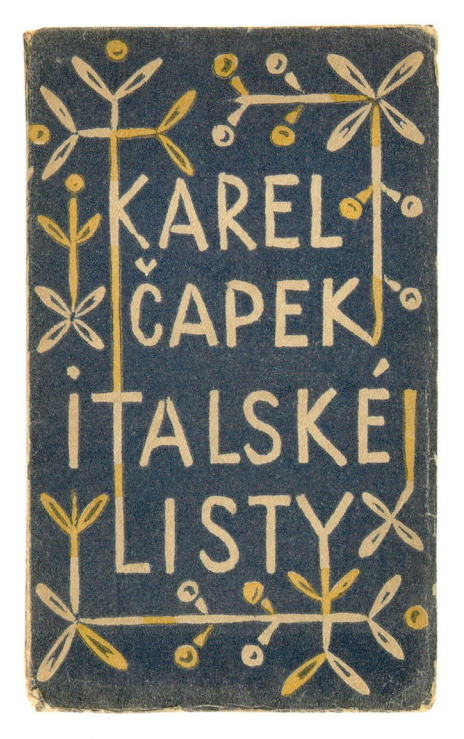

62

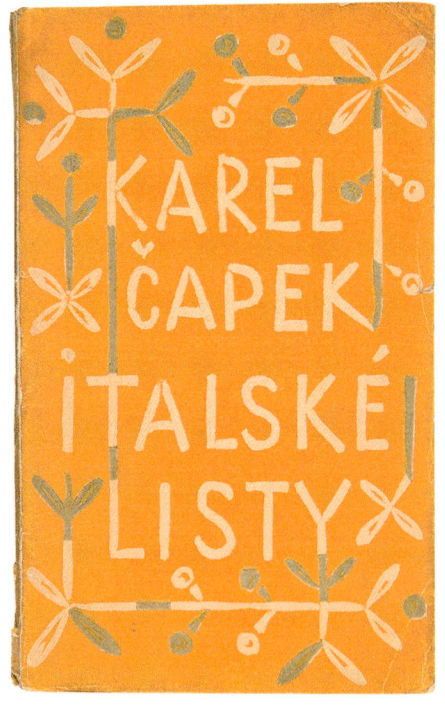

Italské listy / Karel Čapek
Letters from Italy / Karel Čapek
イタリアからの手紙 / カレル・チャペック
1st ed. / 初版
1923

Italské listy / Karel Čapek
Letters from Italy / Karel Čapek
イタリアからの手紙 / カレル・チャペック
2nd ed. / 2版
1924

63

40

Italské listy / Karel Čapek
Letters from Italy / Karel Čapek
イタリアからの手紙 / カレル・チャペック
3rd ed. / 3版
1925

Italské listy / Karel Čapek
Letters of Italy / Karel Čapek
イタリアからの手紙 / カレル・チャペック
4th ed. / 4版
1926

65

Občanská válka / Jiří Haussman
Civil War / Jiří Haussman
市民戦争 / イジー・ハウスマン
1st ed. / 初版
1923

68

43

Červen / Fráňa Šrámek
June / Fráňa Šrámek
6月 / フラーニャ・シュラーメック
2nd ed. / 2版
1923

Plačící satyr / Fráňa Šrámek
The Crying Satyr / Fráňa Šrámek
泣いているサテュロス / フラーニャ・シュラーメック
1st ed. / 初版
1923

Objevy / Charles Vidlrac
Discoveries / Charles Vidlrac
発見 / シャルル・ヴィルドゥラック
1st ed. / 初版
1923

71

72

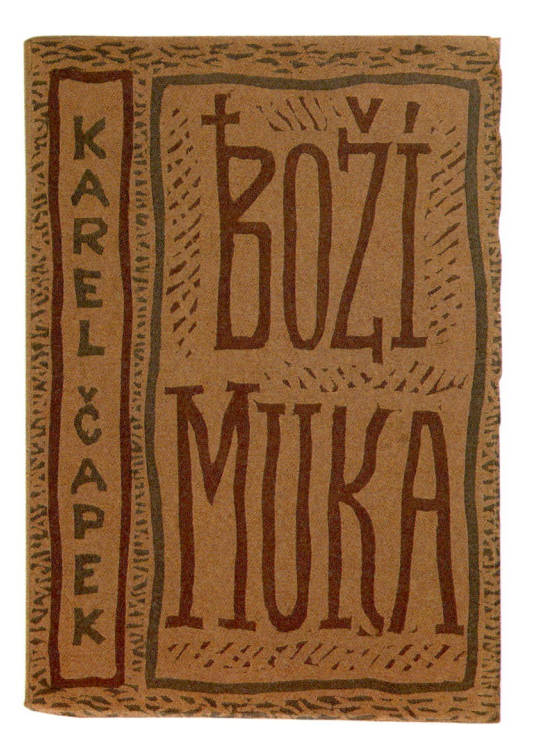

Boží muka / Karel Čapek
Wayside Column / Karel Čapek
受難像 / カレル・チャペック
2nd ed. / 2版
1924

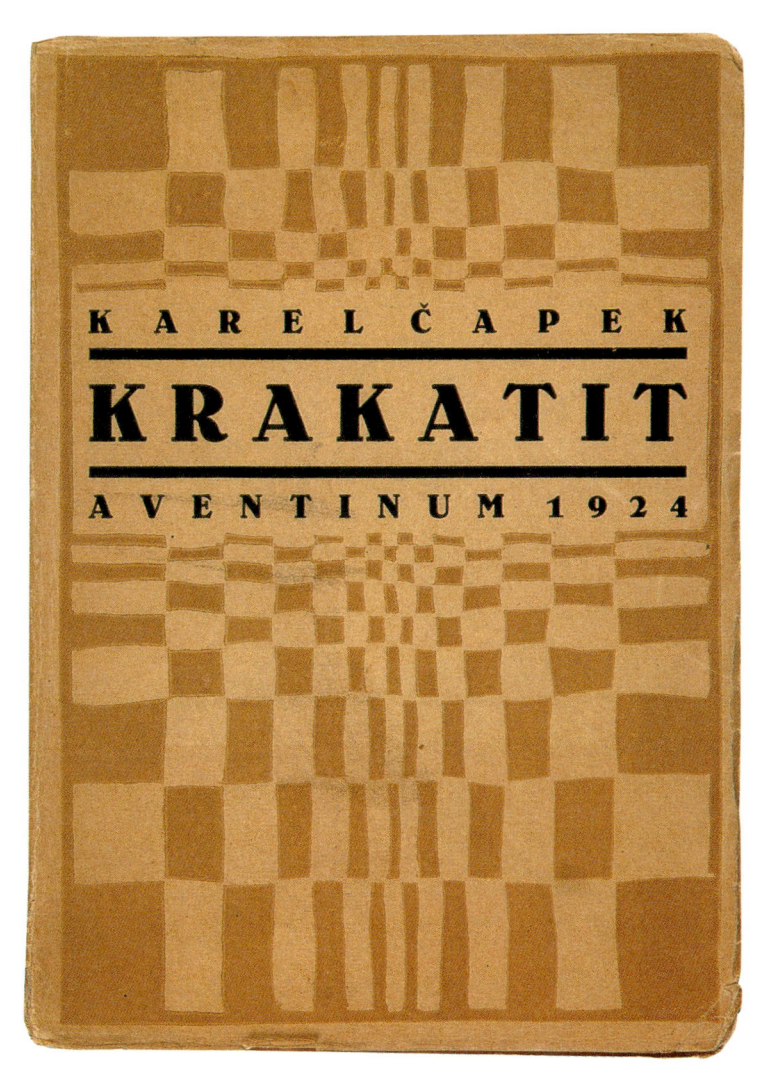

Krakatit / Karel Čapek
Krakatit / Karel Čapek
クラカチット / カレル・チャペック
1st ed. / 初版
1924

74

FU / František Kubka
FU / František Kubka
FU / フランチシェク・クブカ
1st ed. / 初版
1924

75

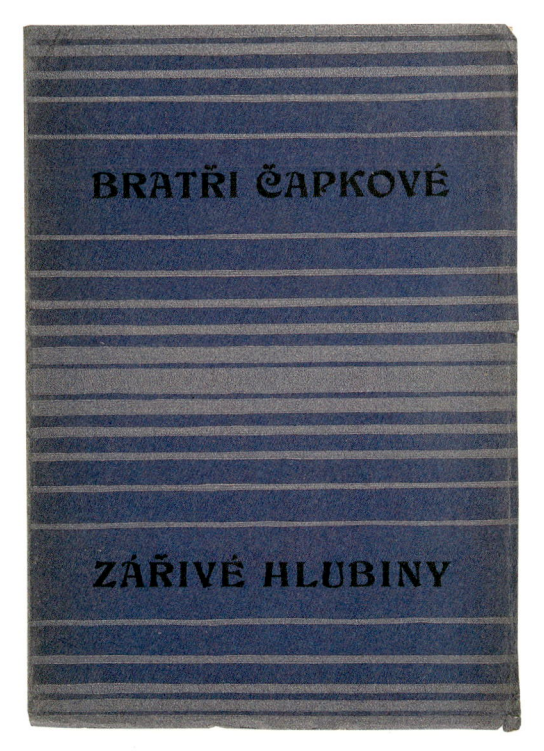

Zářivé hlubiny a jiné prosy / Bratří Čapkové
The Shining Depths and Other Stories / Josef & Karel Čapek
輝く深淵と他の物語 / チャペック兄弟
2nd ed. / 2版
1924

76

Knížka o českém charakteru / Jiří Mahen
On Czech Characteristics / Jiří Mahen
チェコ的特徴についての本 / イジー・マヘン
1st ed. / 初版
1924

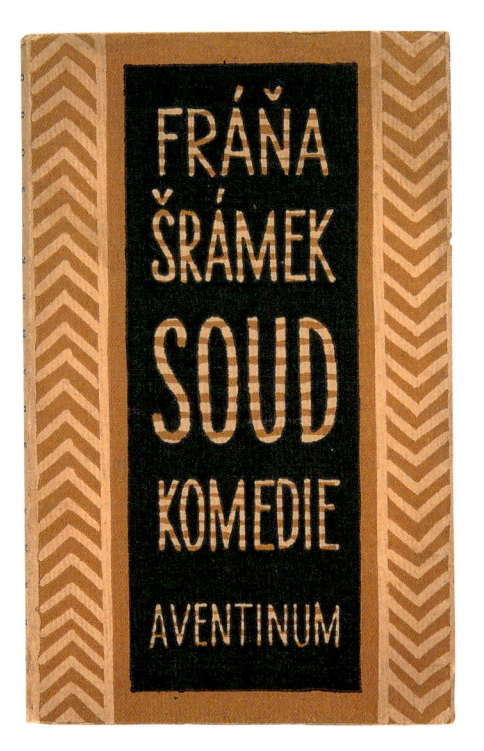

Soud / Fráňa Šrámek
The Judgement / Fráňa Šrámek
判決 / フラーニャ・シュラーメック
1st ed. / 初版
1924

79

Zloděj z Bagdadu / Konstantin Biebl
Thief from Baghdad / Konstantin Biebl
バグダッドの盗賊 / コンスタンチン・ビーブル
1st ed. / 初版
1925

Měsíční vitriol / Henri Béraud
Vitriol of the Moon / Henri Béraud
月の硫酸塩 / アンリ・ベロー
1st ed. / 初版
1925

81

Anglické listy

Karel Čapek's experiences in England, particularly London, and Scotland.
With numerous illustrations by the author.

カレル・チャペックのイギリス旅行記。ロンドンを中心に英国と、
スコットランドでの体験記。カレルの手によるイラストが多数含まれる。

KAREL ČAPEK

ANGLICKÉ
LISTY

ČTVRTÉ VYDÁNÍ

AVENTINUM PRAHA

84

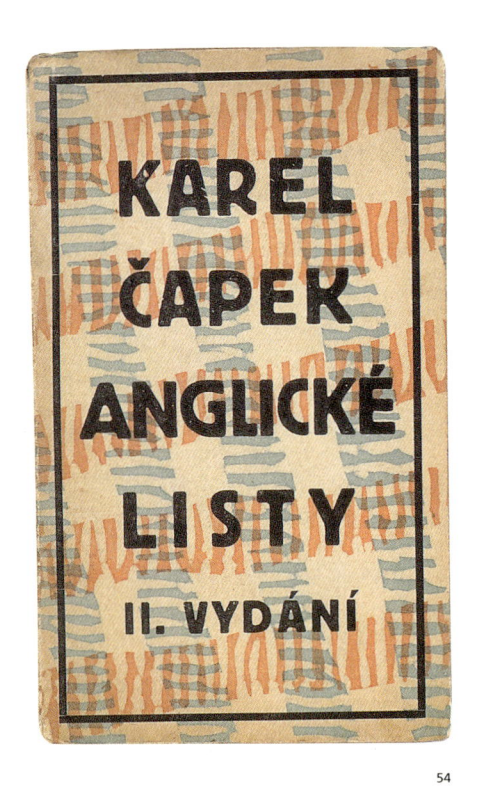

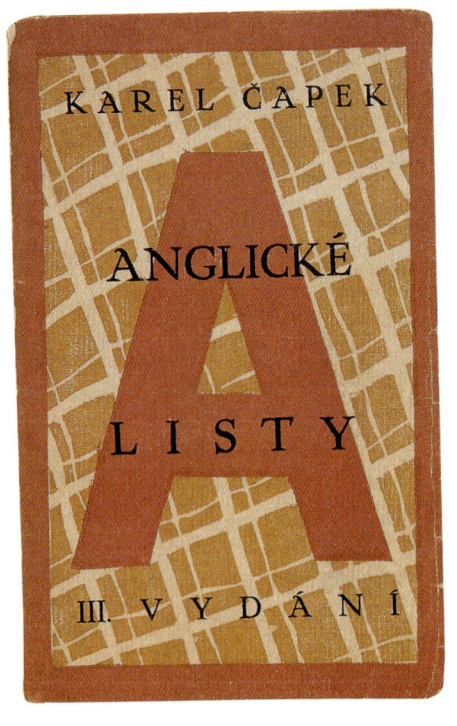

Anglické listy / Karel Čapek
Letters from England / Karel Čapek
イギリス便り / カレル・チャペック
2nd ed. / 2版
1925

Anglické listy / Karel Čapek
Letters from England / Karel Čapek
イギリス便り / カレル・チャペック
3rd ed. / 3版
1925

85

KAREL ČAPEK

ANGLICKÉ

A

LISTY

ČTVRTÉ VYDÁNÍ

AVENTINUM PRAHA

Anglické listy / Karel Čapek
Letters from England / Karel Čapek
イギリス便り / カレル・チャペック
4th ed. / 4版
1927

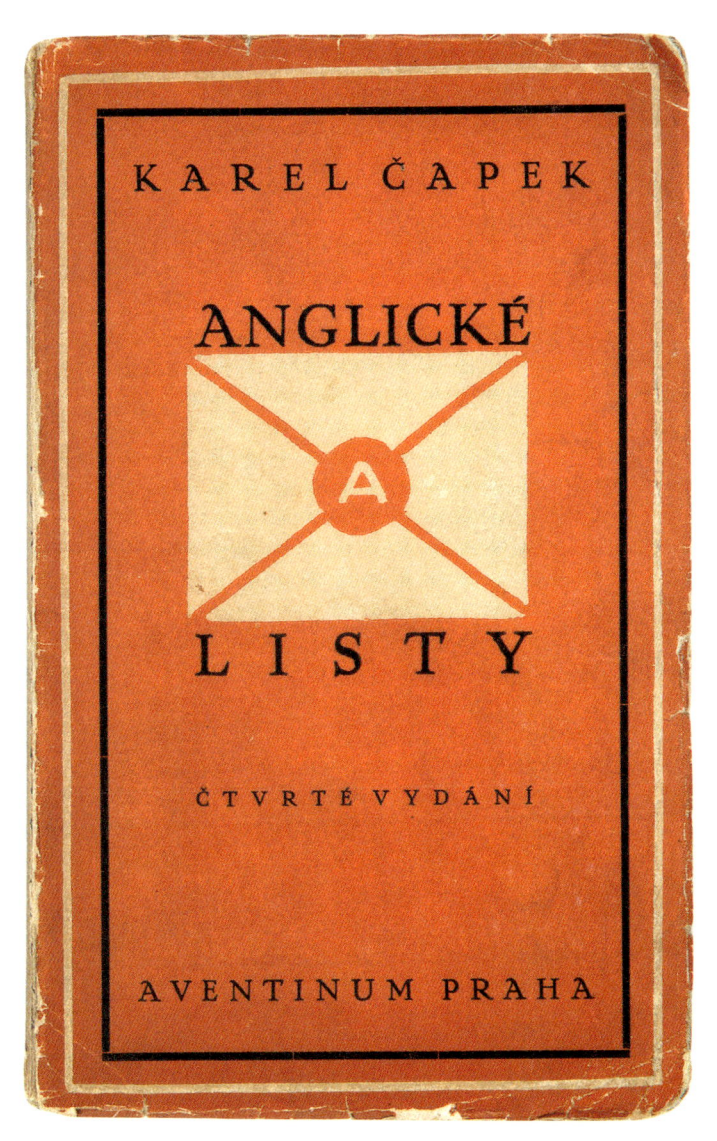

Noc / František Langer
Night / František Langer
夜 / フランチシェク・ラングル
1st ed. / 初版
1925

87

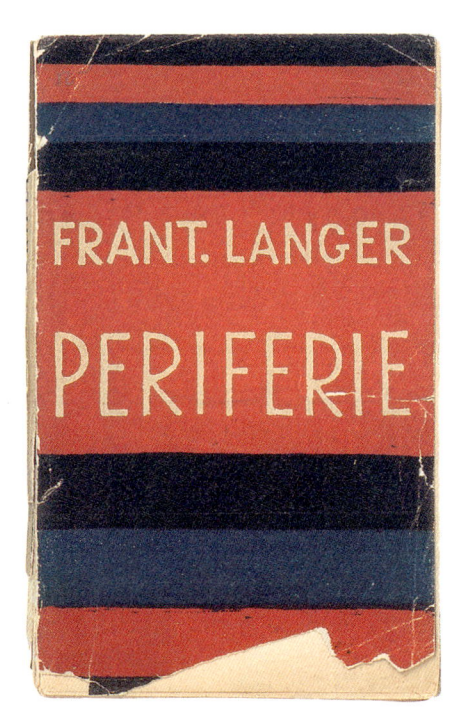

Válčení civilistovo / Stanislav Kostka Neumann
Civilian's War / Stanislav Kostka Neumann
市民の戦争 / スタニスラフ・コストカ・ノイマン
1st ed. / 初版
1925

Periferie / František Langer
Periphery / František Langer
郊外 / フランチシェク・ラングル
1st ed. / 初版
1925

88

V ponorkovém pásmu / Eugéne O'Neill
In the Zone / Eugéne O'Neill
喫水線で / ユージン・オニール
1st ed. / 初版
1925

90

O nejbližších věcech / Karel Čapek
Intimate Things / Karel Čapek
最も身近なものについて / カレル・チャペック
1st ed. / 初版
1925

KAREL ČAPEK

O NEJBLIŽŠÍCH VĚCECH

II. VYDÁNÍ

NAKLADATELSTVÍ AVENTINUM PRAHA

O nejbližších věcech / Karel Čapek
Intimate Things / Karel Čapek
最も身近なものについて / カレル・チャペック
2nd ed. / 2版
1927

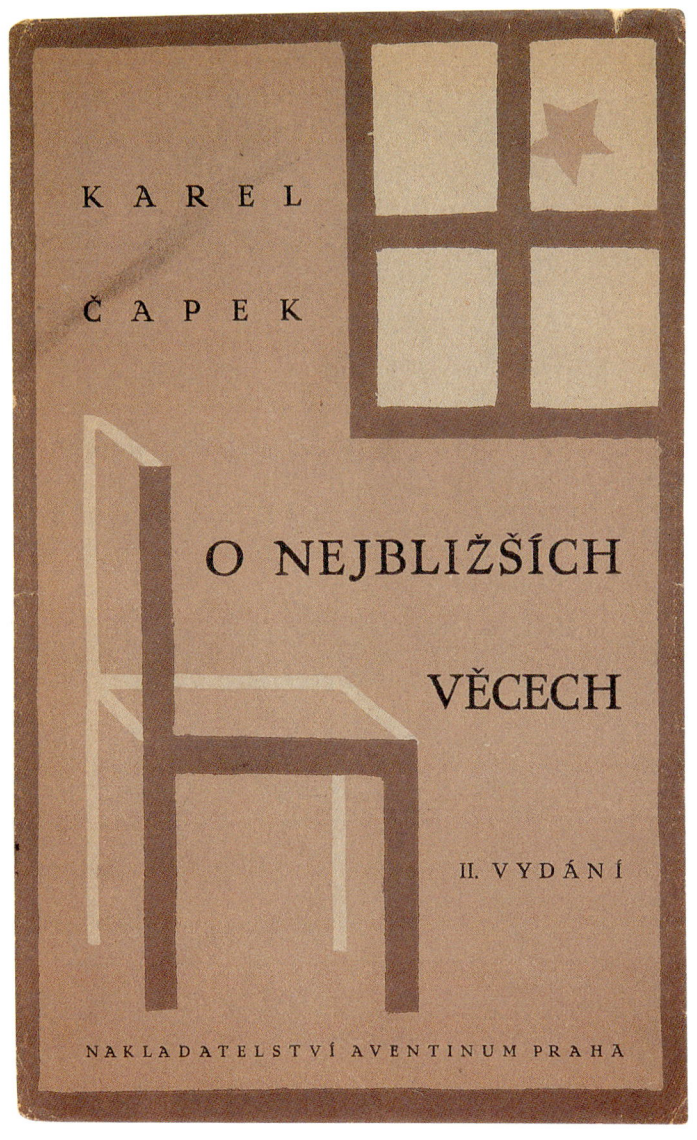

Probuzeni / Josef Hora
Awakening / Josef Hora
目覚め / ヨゼフ・ホラ
1st ed. / 初版
1925

Lidumil na kříži / Čestmír Jeřábek
Philanthropist on the Cross / Čestmír Jeřábek
十字架の上の博愛主義者 / チェストミール・イェジャーベック
1st ed. / 初版
1925

Člověk v zoologické zahradě

Fiction. Translaed by K. Klaus. After his girlfriend, in a fit of rage,
tells him he should be in the zoo,
a man moves into a cage between an oran-utan
and chimpanzee and becomes a popular attraction.

小説　K.クラウス訳
恋人とけんかをして、彼女から「動物園にずっといればいい」と言われた男が
オラウータンとチンパンジーの間にある檻の中に入り、動物園の人気者になる。

DAVID GARNETT

ČLOVĚK
V ZOOLOGICKÉ
ZAHRADĚ

1925

96

Člověk v zoologické zahradě / David Garnett
A Man in the Zoo / David Garnett
動物園の人間 / デビッド・ガーネット
1st ed. / 初版
1925

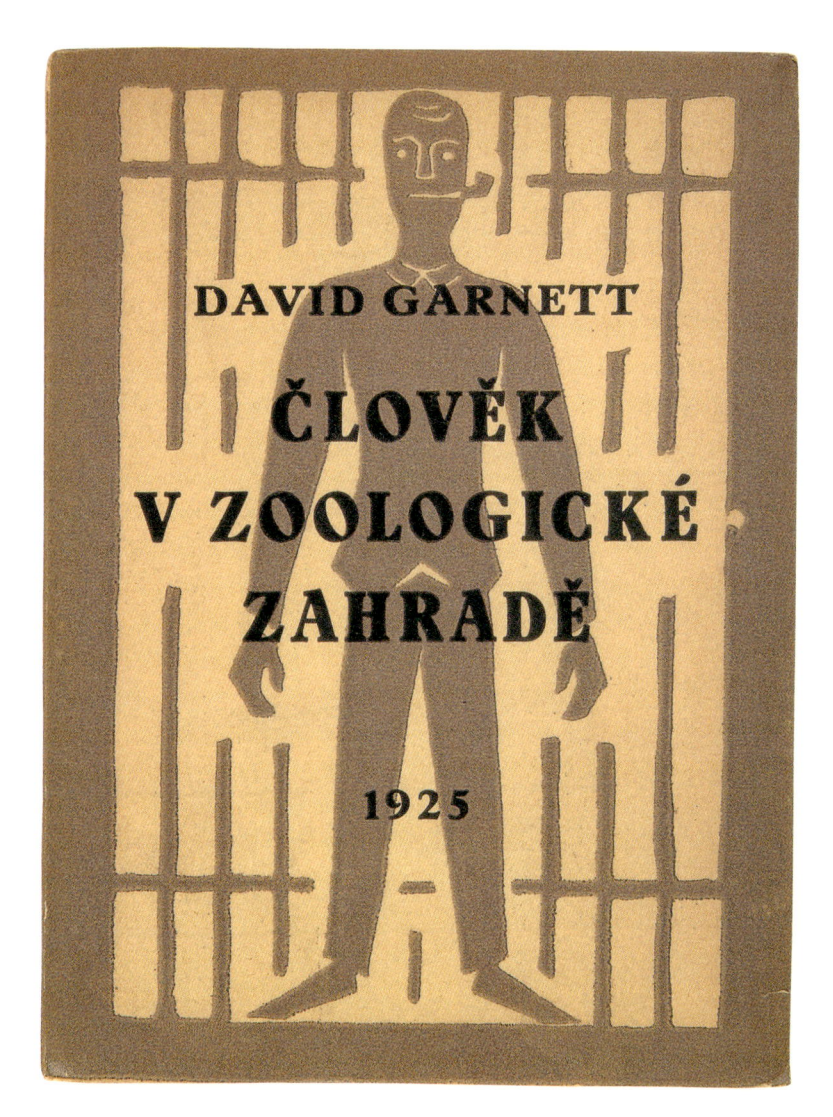

98

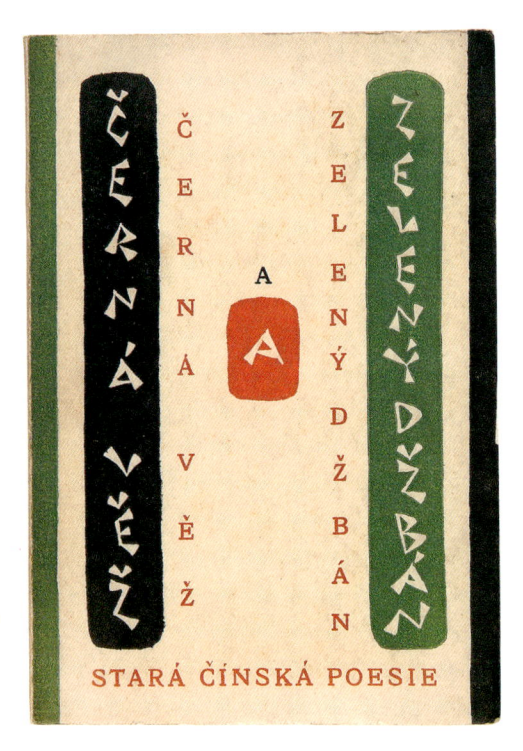

Černá věž a zelený džbán
Black Tower and Green Pitcher
黒い塔と緑の水差し
1st ed. / 初版
1925

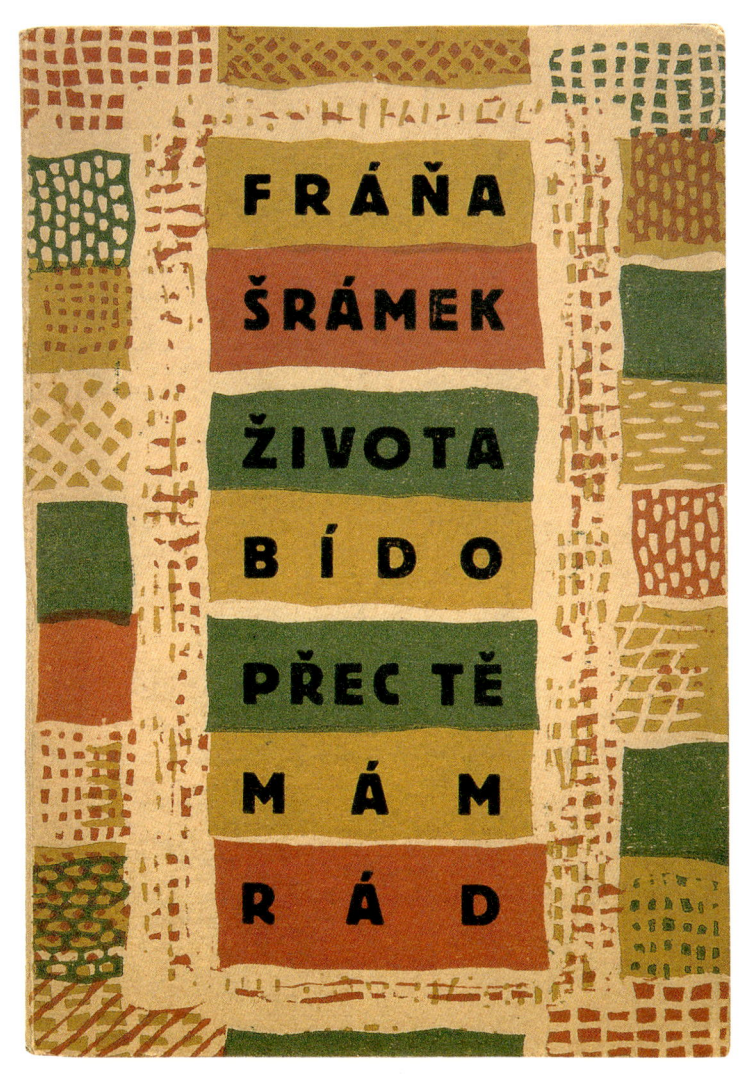

Života bído, přec tě mám rád / Fráňa Šrámek
Life, You're Penury, But I Still Love You / Fráňa Šrámek
生活の貧困よ、それでも私はおまえが好きだ / フラーニャ・シュラーメック
1st ed. / 初版
1924

100

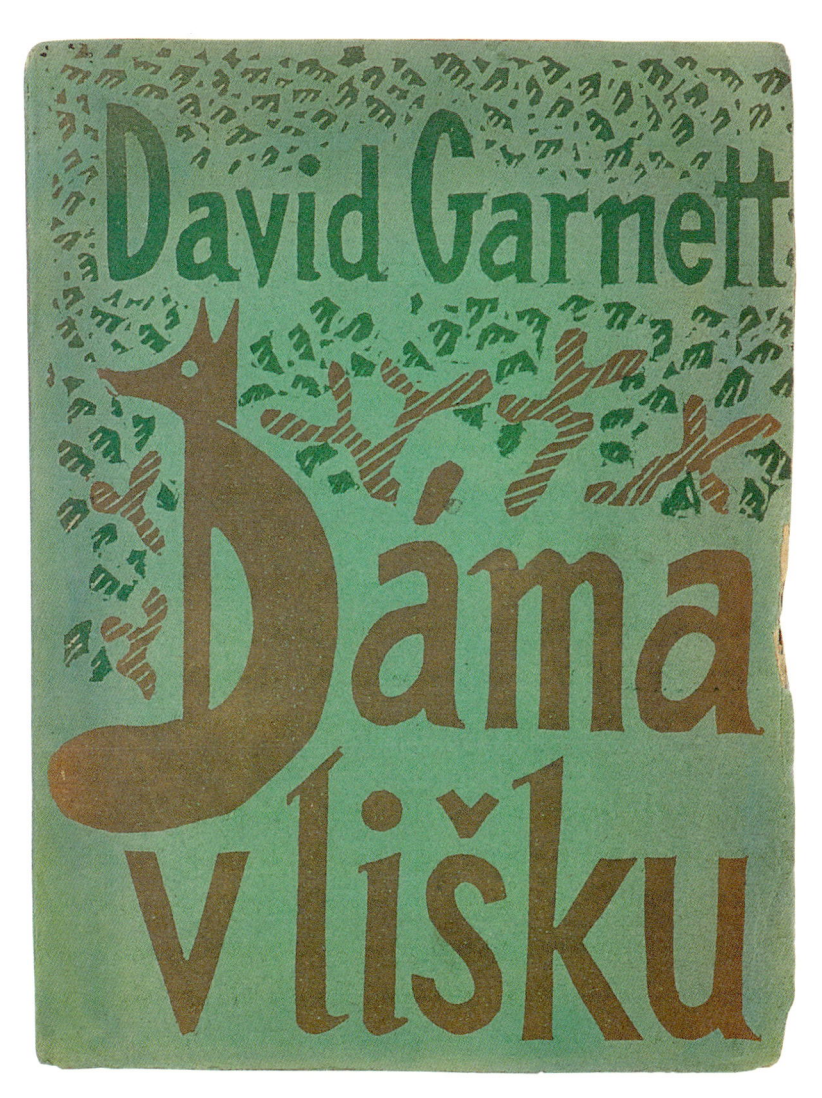

Dáma v lišku / David Garnett
Lady into Fox / David Garnett
キツネになった貴婦人 / デビッド・ガーネット
1st ed. / 初版
1925

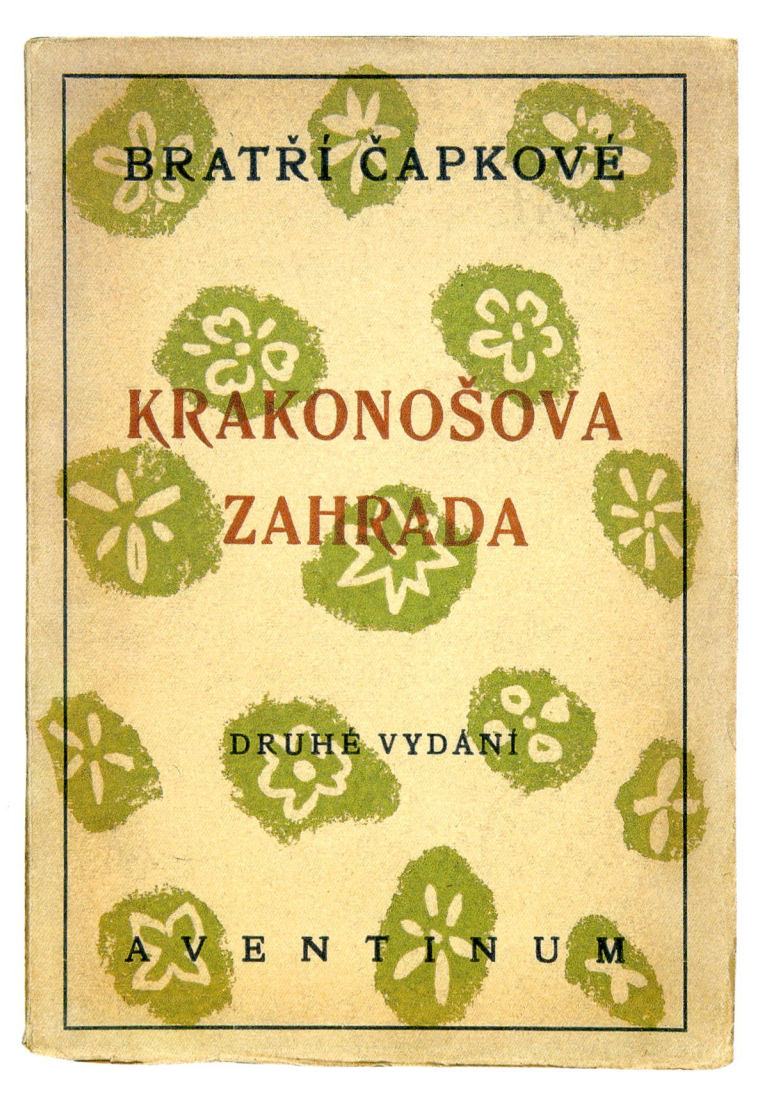

Krakonošova zahrada / Bratrí Čapkové
Krakonoš's Garden / Josef & Karel Čapek
クラコノシュの庭 / チャペック兄弟
2nd ed. / 2版
1926

103

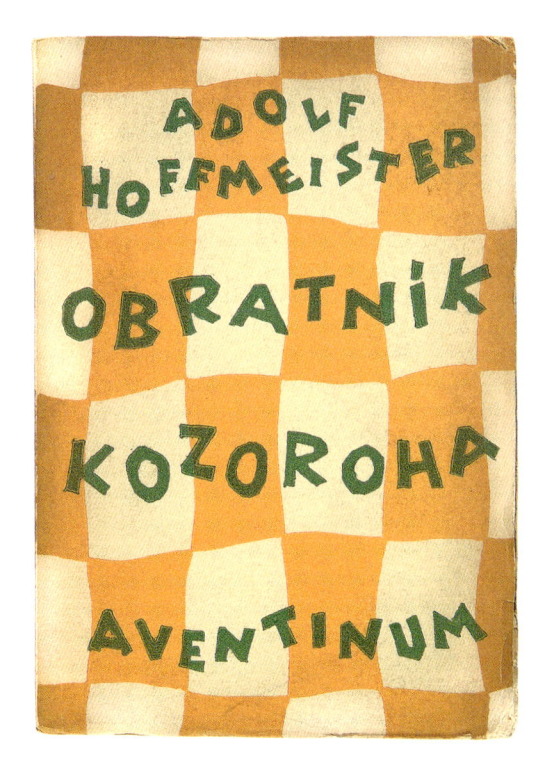

70

Obratnik kozoroha / Adolf Hoffmeister
Tropic of Capricorn / Adolf Hoffmeister
南回帰線 / アドルフ・ホフマイステル
1st ed. / 初版
1926

104

本の表紙
ヨゼフ・チャペック

　私がここで本の表紙について述べたいと思っていることが、何とはなしに一般化されることを私は望まない。近年はこの分野で一連の多方面におよぶ解決策や刺激がもたらされ、新しい本のグラフィック・アートの本当に豊かな文化が発展した。しかし、ここで私が何か話すことができるとしたら、それはまず私の個人的な経験についてで、この新しい本の文化のごく限られた一部分である。そもそものところ私はプロのグラフィック・アーティストではなく、たまたまこの領域にまったくの偶然から入ったのである。私がこの仕事を長く続けられていたとしたら、思いがけず、そして――私は告白するが――望まれもしないのに、私が個人的に役に立てるという、ありがたい活動分野が驚いたことにここに突然、私に対して開かれたというのがその理由である。
　ところでもっともプリミティブで、しかも、もっとも貧困な発端から、まさにその問題は始まった。印刷の技術においても戦争※1の影響で依然としてわれわれにとって非常にはっきりと感じられる物価高が残っているその時代に、私にまかされたのは安く上がる表紙を作ることであり、打出し印刷や多色といった費用のかかることはさけなければならなかった。そこで私はリノリウム※2を彫る方法を選んだ。というのは、いずれにせよリノリウムの古い板に彫られた表紙が耐えられないほど本の値段を高くするだろうということは予想しえなかったからである（それは今もありえない）。
　もちろんのこと私は、使用や圧力に一番容易に耐えられるような、大きくて粗い平面を選ぶことに解決策を見出した。すなわち、リノリウムの使用はここでは単純で、やむを得ずとられたテクニックではあるが、それを使った最初のときから、一定の独特な有利さがあることがわかった。まずこのようなリノリウムの板は面全体を根本から支配し、それを一気にすぐ大きな枠どりで分割し、着色することができる。たとえばこれが打出し印刷のための線描きのデッサンでは、きっとある種の薄さやおとなしさがでて、あまり大胆な構成をしないようにと誘導されてしまうことであろう。このことにより、他の人たちや他の場所で見出されているような

本の表紙に対する近代的な解決方法への同意につながる特別な道が与えられた。明らかにちゃんとした表紙というものは前もって全体として統制して作られるように要請されている。

それは絵と枠と文字がそれぞれバラバラに分解されるようなことがあってはならず、むしろ絵というより、物というか一つのまとまった対象となるように統一的な性格によってコントロールされていなければならない。表紙において、本を独特な有機体、物、あるいは、対象となしえているものは、絵でもなければ、紋章でもない。表紙というものはいつも、もし何かによって飾られていないなら、デッサンされた平面として残るのである。この原則は単に区分だけではなく、色彩にも及び、色彩もまた表紙の基本的な表現を十分に構成し、ただ色をつけるという二次的な目的に役立つだけであってはならない。

以上、本の表紙の外的な技術的特徴一般についてはこれだけ述べておこう。しかし、技術と同様に重要な要素は個々の一つ一つのケースや作品それぞれの内的な本質について適切な表現を与えるという課題の解決である。詩の本や、皮肉に富む小説や、あるいは悲劇の表紙の作り方は同じではない。エレガントな軽快さで書く著者の作品と、あるいはぎっしりと、暗い感じで書く著者の作品とでは語りかける表紙の内容は同じではない。そして、すでに本のタイトルそのものがその本の本来の名前であり、その本を本来の一個の個性あるものとしている。そこで表紙のタイトルそのものがその本の特徴を非常に本質的に決定していることになる。それどころか時としてあるタイトルの非常な長さ、またはその特別に目に立つ短さがすでにもうその本の方向を定めるものとしてセットされ、それがしばしば表紙を作る最初の構想において構成的な要素としての役割を演ずるのである。

表紙の制作にはその本のタイトルの総体、そしてもちろんより大切なものとして本そのものの内容や特徴が、表紙の考案者に一連の考え、連想、それに示唆を呼びおこすので、それらにできるだけ単純で、明瞭で、適切な表現を与えなければならない。もちろんのこと、本が「雲の中で」、「砂漠からの短編集」、あるいは、「山々にて」などというタイトルであったら、これらの本はわれわれに常に異なった考え、形式的、色彩的、感情的、ダイナミック等々の連想をおこさせる。そこですなわち、それらの夢見るようなぼんやりした頭の中でごちゃまぜになっている考えをしっかりとらえて、それをできるだけ手短に、しかも同時にできるだけ充実した形で、表紙にその本の具体的表現を含むよう、形式的要点をまとめ上げる必要がある。つまりここにはファンタジーと同時に非常に極端な具体性を併せもつことが必要で、そしてそれはもちろん個性化する形式的豊かさへの唯一の道であり、その豊かさ

の中に一つ一つの本が感謝すべき、そして、読み手が決してその本の内容全部を汲みつくせない機会を用意するのである。
　もちろん同様に作品全体としてのよい画像的効果に配慮しなければならない。すなわちテクニックからそのテクニックを導き出した素材の性格と美しさを得て、同時に課題の解決のために、本の表紙をも芸術作品とする、例の非物質的魅力や、特色というものを入れなければならないのである。

※1　ここでは第1次世界大戦のこと。
※2　版画の原版に用いられる材質のひとつで、亜麻仁油、キリ油などと松脂、おがくず、コルク粉などをまぜ、麻布に圧着させたもの。

Book Covers
Josef Čapek

What I would like to say about book covers here should not be taken, by any means, as a generalization. Modern times have brought to this field a versatile range of solutions and a truly rich culture of book covers has emerged. If I should voice my opinions here, they would mostly reflect my own experience in this small part of the new book culture. To begin, graphic art is not my occupation. I actually came upon this profession by chance. I have to admit that the reason I continued in this line of work was mostly because, unexpectedly and unasked for, a surprisingly rewarding field of work opened up for me—a field in which I found I was able to fulfill myself.

It all started from the most primitive and poorest of beginnings. The war #1 had left behind high prices that were clearly seen in the costs of printing, and I was entrusted to create book covers that were inexpensive. It was necessary to work without printing blocks or multicolor prints because of their high cost. I chose to work with linoleum #2. We did not have to worry that the editions of books we were printing would run to such a large number that the design cut into a piece of old linoleum would not hold up.

Of course, I opted for answers using large, rough areas that better resisted the usage and pressure of printing. And there the technique, though primitive and chosen out of need, immediately demonstrated its extraordinary character. Linoleum panels radically dominate the whole printing area. They divide it and color it at the same time, and do so boldly. Linear painting for printing blocks, by contrast, would rather seduce the artist into certain restrictions, more timid, and with a less comprehensive composition. Thus, a distinctive way for creating book covers was established. It falls in line with a modern approach to book covers that can be found in other works elsewhere. Without a doubt, the true book cover wants to dominate and be created as a whole.

It should not fall into separate parts—illustration, frame and letters—but should exhibit a unifying character so it becomes a complete object rather than a picture. Because it is neither picture nor ornament, what is on the cover turns the book into an individual organism, a thing, an object; if decorations are added only to the book cover, then it remains nothing more than a painted area. This policy does not extend just to the composition of the cover, but also to the colors. The colors should fully conform to the fundamental expression of the cover, and should not be used for subsidiary coloring.

That all refers to the outward, technical aspect of book covers. The same importance is given to the task of giving an individual cover inner substance specific to each case or each work. It is not the same working on book covers for collections of poetry, satirical novels or tragedies. It is not the same creating a book cover for an author who writes with light elegance, as for an author whose writing is dark and dense. The title of a book already provides it with a personal name and creates its own individuality. In the same way, the text of a book cover appoints an essential character to it. The foundation for this character is found there, in the text of the title. Sometimes in its considerable length, and other times in its exceptional briefness, it very often plays the role of a component of the composition from the first plan. The content and character of the book itself, of course, elicit a range of images and associations for the creator of the book cover. It is essential to give these images the most simple, most pragmatic and clearest expression, entirely distinct from associations that are formal, colorful, emotional or dynamic. It is not necessary to hold on tight to any dreamy, wandering confusion of images and assemble them into a formal abbreviation that would briefly, but at the same time comprehensively embrace the objective content of the book on its cover. What is needed here is fantasy, combined with a very extreme sense of objectivity. That is the only way to express the individual wealth that each book offers of grateful, inexhaustible opportunity.

Still it is necessary to bear in mind the positive graphic effect of the entire work. That means drawing beauty from the technical nature of the material and concurrently endowing an immaterial grace to the task, a distinction that makes the book cover into a work of art.

#1 The First World War.
#2 A material used for printing plates. Sawdust or powdered cork is mixed with linseed oil and pine resin, pressed flat and hardened on a hemp base.

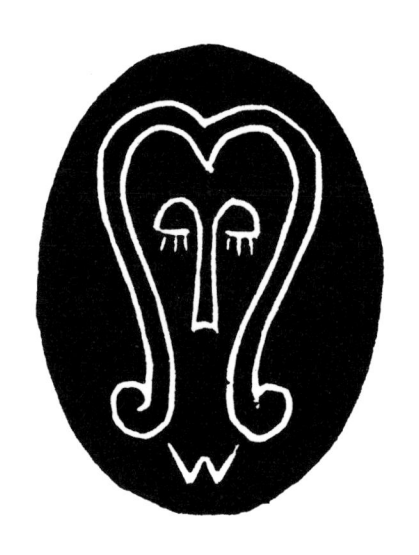

114

本の表紙はどのように作るか
ヨゼフ・チャペック

　この一文のタイトルを見たら、多くの人が「おい。あいつお高くとまっちゃって、作り方の規則を決めようとしている。」と、言うであろう。というのも、もしこのテーマで誰か文を書いてはいけない人間がいるとしたら、運命のいたずらによって望む以上に多くの本の表紙を作るよう任された私こそが、まさにそれにあてはまるだろうからだ。しかし、この雑誌※1の編集者はまるで死のように避けがたいものとして長年、本の表紙についての記事で私を苦しめようと目論んでいて、それをどうやって片付けたらいいのか、もうほかに手段が考えつかないのである。
　この一文の冒頭ではっきり宣言しておくが、「本の表紙はどのように作るか」など、私は知らない。本の表紙はありとあらゆる方法で作り、そこには何ひとつ統一的な特徴や法則はない。私に関して言えば、自分の仕事からでも何ひとつ処方箋なりレシピなり、一般的法則をも引き出すことはできなかった。誰でもここではできるだけのことをするし、自分に要求されていることをする。そして、本のグラフィック・アートの専門家のタイトルにふさわしい人の手でなされるのがここでもっとも考慮されるべきである、というのが一番正しい。
　私自身は（まず第一に）いつも自分をただひたすら画家であると感じていて、一度もグラフィック・アーティストだと思ったことはない。私にとってもなんらの期待もしていず、そして、そもそもなんらの功名心もないのに創造面で表現することができ、役にたてられる可能性を与えられた分野がまさか本のグラフィック・アートになろうとは、私自身、一度だって思ってもみなかった。私がそれに偶然にかかわりあうことになったとき、私にはもろもろの前提になる知識も情報もなく、あらゆる原則も欠けているうえ、それに加えて一定の、かなりの量のアナーキズムがあった。告白しないといけないが、愛書家用の版、模範的で、見事になされた印刷が私を特に喜ばせたことは一度もなかったし、それらについての記事を私はいつも下品な肌合いの、ある種の笑いとともに読んできた。というのもその記事を見るとどうしても晴れ着について大げさに表現したダンスパーティーの記事を思い出し

てしまうからである。今日でも依然として極度に繊細で、折衷的に上品な飾りのついた本を手にするとき、これは私の趣味ではないという絶ち難い思いにかられる。ごらんの通り、私は本のグラフィック・アートにはごく僅かしかお呼びではないし、あらかじめ自分の行く道がそこに決められていた訳ではない。

　私が初めてパリに行ったとき、アルカンやフラマリオン、その他の安価な版の統一された表紙は、その部数の多さと個々の単純な装丁で、これこそ一番正しいものだと私には思え、大きな印象を私に与えた。これこそ一番正しい！と私は考えた。しかし当時私は、本の条件はどこでも同じではないということを、何となく意識していなかった。これらは古参の出版社で、その版は長いこと使われているが、わが国では新しい、若い出版社こそがもっとも元気のいい出版社で、これらの出版社は多くの場合近代的な読者に食い込み、それにあまりポピュラーでない文学を扱う。そしてその他、わが国では本は通常それほど少なくない出版部数で出されており、そんな訳で、書籍市場にはいつもあまり成功していない本や有名な人の本がたくさん現れるので、新しい若い出版社は非常にはっきりと注意をひくようにしなければならない。

　これらのことが私の統一性への好みを、一つ一つの本にはその独自の表現、特別で異なった魅力や形を与えるべきだという確信へと向けさせた。わが国の書店のウィンドウを見てみれば、そこでは一冊の本がもう一冊を飛び越えて声をあげ、一冊がもう一冊をやっつけ、打ち破ろうとし、新しい一冊一冊が、もう一週間前に出たものをつついて追い出そうと努める。ここではすなわち、このゲームで本同士はいつも力強い証拠でお互いを打ち破らねばならない。今日の本は、戦前に出版された本と比べてすでに明らかにかなり違って見える。以前は本の表紙には絵が、あるいはもっとよい場合には繊細なデザインがあった。今日ではもう明らかなように、新しい表紙には本質的に新しい宣伝がやってきた。最近若い本の装丁家の一人が、彼の考えによれば近代的な表紙はポスターでなければならないと宣言した。うん、その点で私はもっと先へ行き、ポスターは近代的なポスターであるべきで、本は近代的な本であるべきだといいたい。本屋のウィンドウではせめて――まさに近代的な表紙が、近代的な本にその外的な性格や形を与えるのである。

※１「Pritomnost」…チェコの雑誌のひとつ。
　　「Pritomnost」は日本語で「現代」という意味。

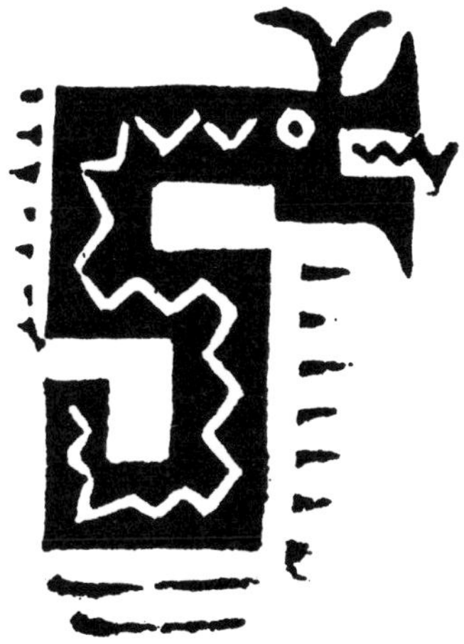

How to Make Book Jackets
Josef Čapek

Seeing the title of this article, many people might be inclined to say, 'Hey, this fellow's a bit presumptuous, thinking he can set the rules!' For if ever there were a person who shouldn't be writing on this subject, that person is me, who by a trick of fate has been asked to make more book jackets than anyone could wish. But the editor of this magazine #1 has long planned to torture me into writing this article, which is as hard as death itself to avoid, and finally I can think of no other way of getting out of it.

I'd like to make it clear from the start that I really don't know 'how to make book jackets'. They are created by every imaginable method, and there's no consistent feature or principle in it anywhere. For myself, I have not been able to draw from my work any prescription or 'recipe', or any general principles. I do what anyone would do in this situation — I do what is requested of me. Ideally for this task the person considered should be the person most suited to the title of graphic artist specializing in book design.

For myself, first and foremost I feel that I am simply a painter, and I have never thought of myself as a graphic artist. With no expectation and no fundamental desire for fame on my part, I never once dreamed that the field in which my creative expression would be put to use would turn out to be graphic art for book design. I became involved almost by chance, having none of the prerequisite knowledge or information, and lacking all formal principles, and in addition bringing to it quite a heavy dose of anarchism. I have to confess that no collector's edition, no superb printing — a model of its kind — has ever once really excited me, and I always read articles about such things with a rude guffaw. The exaggerated language reminds me of the way they describe the fancy clothes people wear to parties. Even today, when I have in my hand a book with extremely delicate and refined decorative details, I still succumb to a persistent feeling that it is not to my taste. As you can see, I was hardly the type to work in graphic art for books, nor was it something I set out to do.

When I first went to Paris I was greatly impressed by the standardized jackets of the low priced editions such as Arkan and Flammarion. I thought that with their large print runs and simple bindings they had the perfect answer. This is how it should be done! I thought. But at that time I wasn't really conscious of the fact that circumstances affecting books were not the same everywhere. Those old-established publishing companies have used those editions for a long time. But in my country, it is the young publishers that are the most active, and many of them have a strong following among modern readers, and they handle the less popular forms of literature. Also in my country, print runs are relatively speaking quite large, and the book market is always full of books—some that are not so successful and some by famous people, so new publishers must work extremely hard to attract attention.

This realization turned me from my love of standardization to a conviction that each and every book should be given a unique style, a special, individual appeal. If you look at the windows of bookshops in my country, you'll see books shouting, jumping over each other, assailing each other. In the fight for attention, every new book struggles to kick aside the books that came out the week before. In other words, this is a game in which you have to attack with powerful visual justification. Already, books look very different these days from those published before the war. Previously there was a picture, or better still some fine design on a book's cover. Now it's very clear that the new jackets bear an essentially new message. Recently a young book designer declared that the way he thought, modern book jackets must act as posters. I agree. In fact, I would go even further and say that the poster should be a modern poster and the book a modern book. At least in the windows of bookshops, modern book jackets are the external expression of the nature and style of modern books.

#1 A Czech magazine entitled 'Pritomnost' (Contemporary Times)

121

Kapitol / Harvey Fergusson
Capitol Hill / Harvey Fergusson
連邦議会議事堂 / ハーヴェイ・ファーガソン
1st ed. / 初版
1926

123

Města a roky / Konstantin Fedin
Cities and Years / Konstantin Fedin
町と歳月 / コンスタンチン・フェージン
1st ed. / 初版
1926

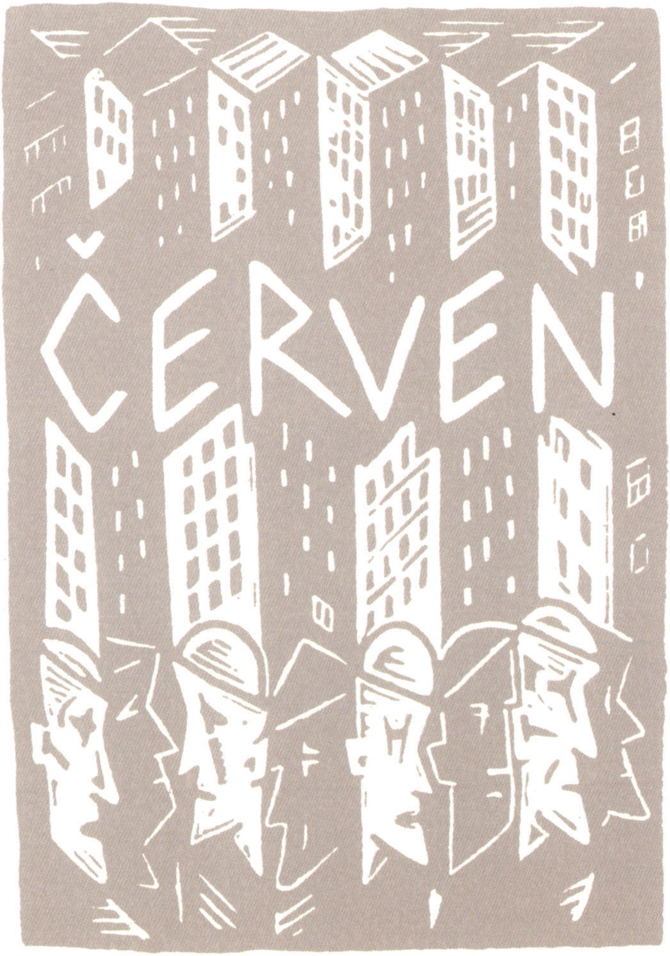
ČERVEN

126

Hlídač č.47 / Josef Kopta
Watchman No 47 / Josef Kopta
線路番No.47 / ヨゼフ・コプタ
1st ed. / 初版
1926

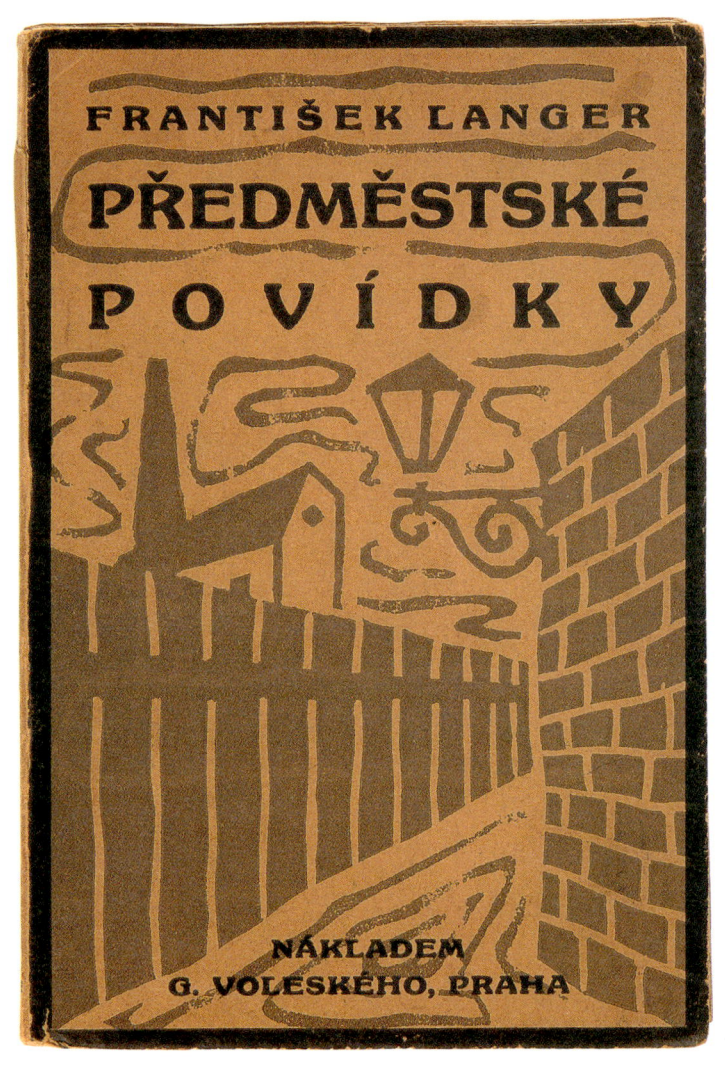

Předměstské povídky / František Langer
Stories from the Suburbs / František Langer
郊外の物語 / フランチシェク・ラングル
1st ed. / 初版
1926

Nebezpečná stáří / Rose Macaulay
Dangerous Ages / Rose Macaulay
危険な老齢 / ローズ・マコーレイ
1st ed. / 初版
1926

Utrpení pětihranného Boba / Jiří Mařánek
Suffering of Pentagonal Bob / Jiří Mařánek
5角形のボブの受難 / イジー・マジャーネック
1st ed. / 初版
1926

郵 便 は が き

170 - 0003

恐れいりますが
切手をお貼り
ください。

東京都豊島区駒込4-14-6 #301
ピエ・ブックス編集部 行

このたびは小社の本をお買い上げいただき、ありがとう存じます。新刊案内の送付と、今後の
企画の参考とさせていただきますので、お手数ですが各欄にご記入の上お送り下さい。

チャペックの本棚
ヨゼフ・チャペックの装丁デザイン

(フリガナ) お名前		年齢	性別 男・女
ご住所　〒　　　　　　　　　　　　TEL　　　　(　　)			
ご職業	購入店名		

● いままでに読者カードをお出しいただいたことが　　1.ある　2.ない

チャペックの本棚 —ヨセフ・チャペックの装丁デザイン— 愛読者カード

1. この本を何でお知りになりましたか。

   1. 新聞・雑誌（紙・誌名　　　　　　　　　　　）　2. チラシ・ポスター
   3. 友人、知人の話　　4. 店頭で見て　　5. プレゼントされた
   6. その他(　　　　　　　　　)

2. この本についてのご意見、ご感想をお聞かせください。

3. 今後、出版物についてどのようなテーマを望まれますか。

4. よく購読される雑誌名をお書きください。

5. 今後、小社より出版をご希望の著者、ジャンル、企画がありましたら、ぜひお聞かせください。

● アンケートにご協力いただきありがとうございました

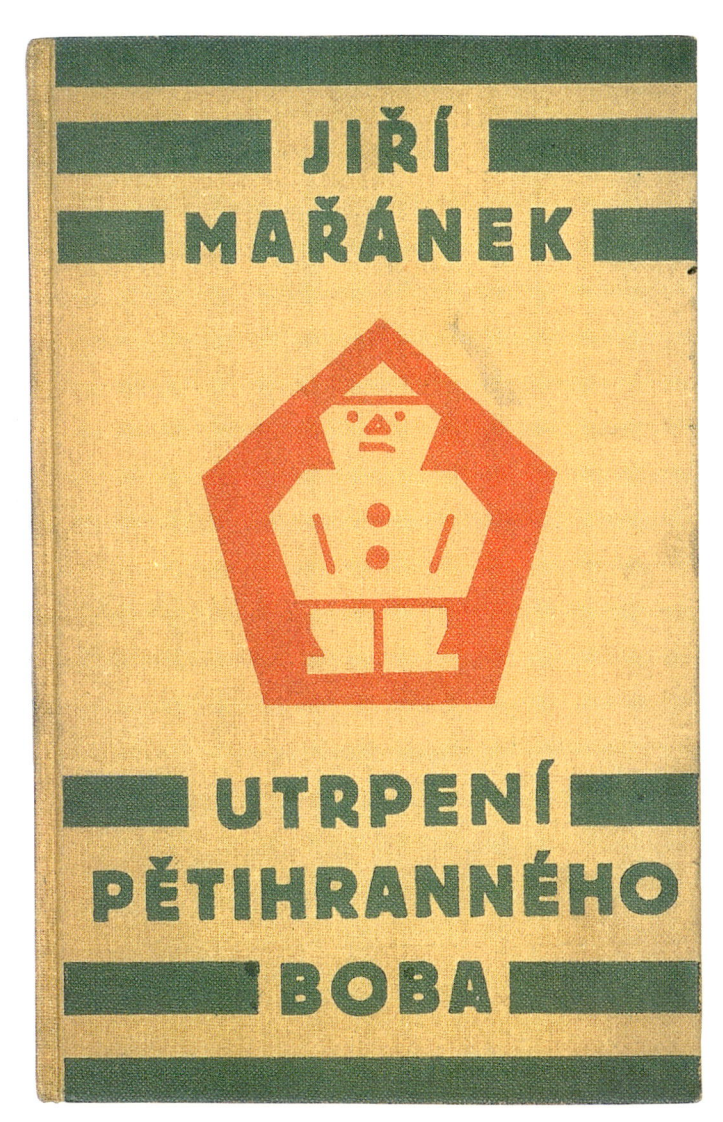

Utrpení pětihranného Boba / Jiří Mařánek
Suffering of Pentagonal Bob / Jiří Mařánek
5角形のボブの受難 / イジー・マジャーネック
Hard bound / ハードカバー
1926

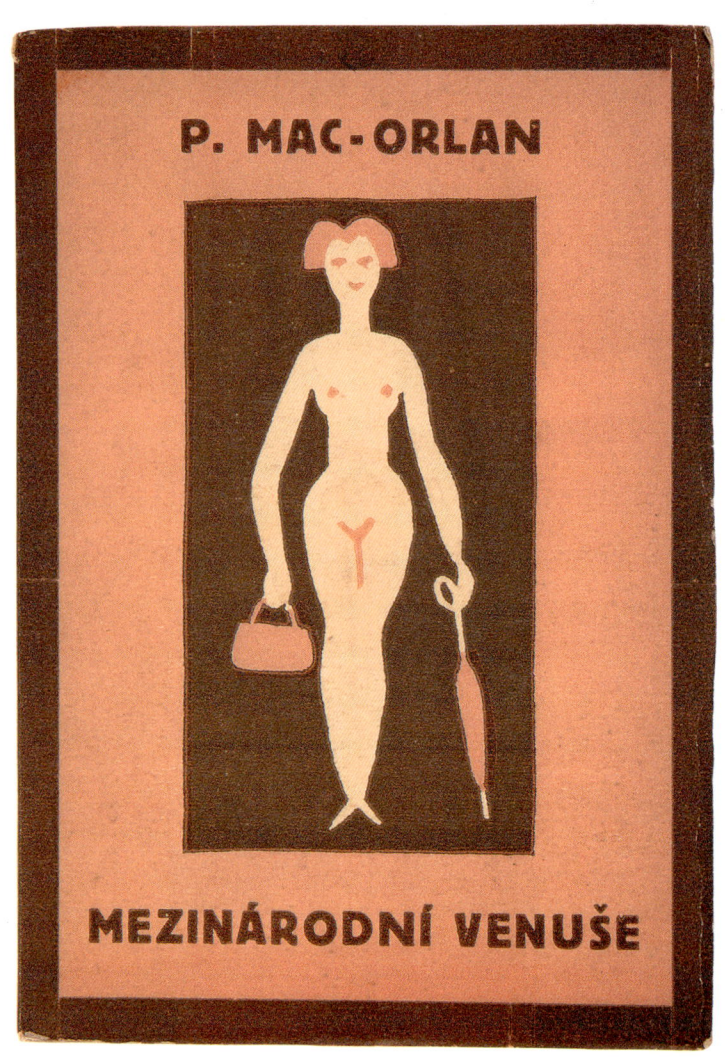

Mezinárodní Venuše / Pierre Mac Orlan
International Venus / Pierre Mac Orlan
国際的なヴィーナス / ピエール・マック・オルラン
1st ed. / 初版
1926

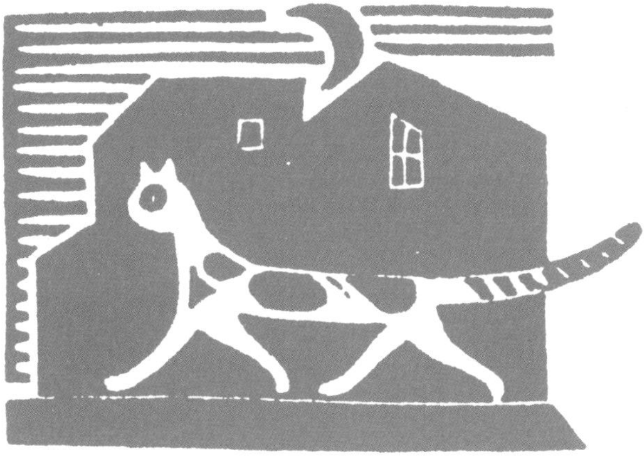

Zlatými Řetězy / Konstantin Biebl
With Chains of Gold / Konstantin Biebl
黄金の鎖で / コンスタンチン・ビーブル
1st ed. / 初版
1926

Jack Spurlock, marnotratný syn / George Horace Lorrimer
Jack Spurlock - Prodigal / George Horace Lorrimer
放蕩息子、ジャック・スパーロック / ジョージ・ホーレス・ロリマー
1st ed. / 初版
1926

Dvojníci a sny / František Kubka
Doppelgängers and Dreams / František Kubka
ドッペルゲンガーと夢 / フランチシェク・クブカ
1st ed. / 初版
1926

Rozmarné léto / Vladislav Vančura
Gay Summer / Vladislav Vančura
陽気な夏 / ヴラジスラフ・ヴァンチュラ
1st ed. / 初版
1926

138

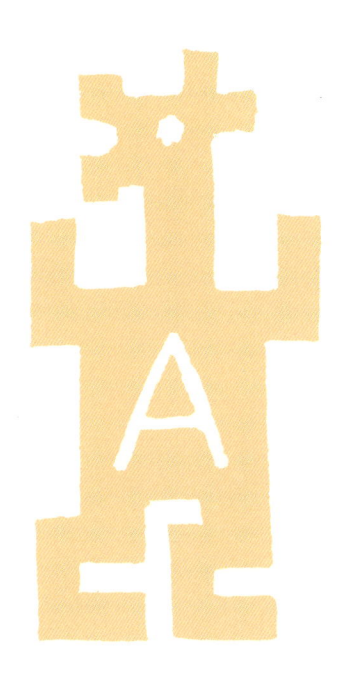

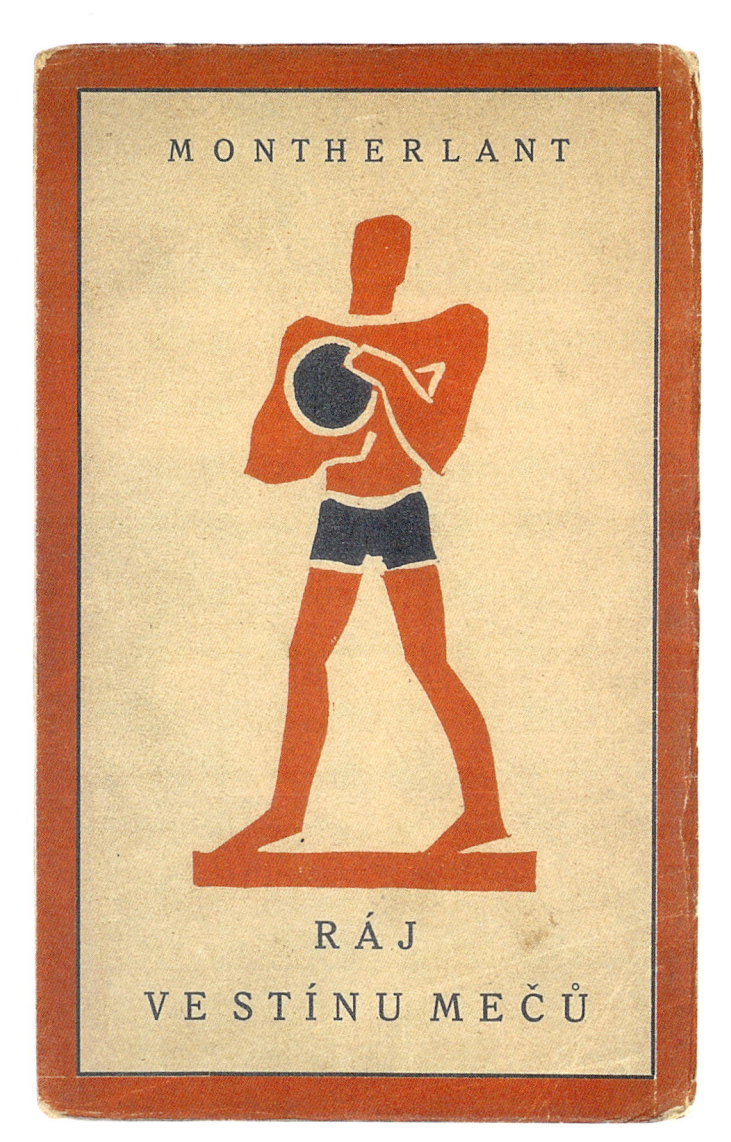

Ráj ve stinu mečů / Henri de Montherlant
Paradise in the Shadow of Swords / Henri de Montherlant
剣の影の楽園 / アンリ・ド・モンテルラン
1st ed. / 初版
1926

140

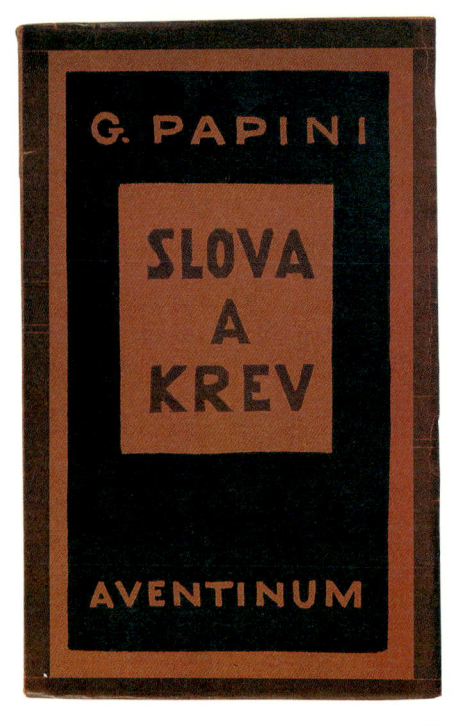

84

85

Slova a krev / Giovanni Papini
Words and Blood / Giovanni Papini
言葉と血 / ジョヴァンニ・パピーニ
1st ed. / 初版
1926

Ostrov veliké lásky / Fráňa Šrámek
Island of Great Love / Fráňa Šrámek
大きな愛の島 / フラーニャ・シュラーメック
1st ed. / 初版
1926

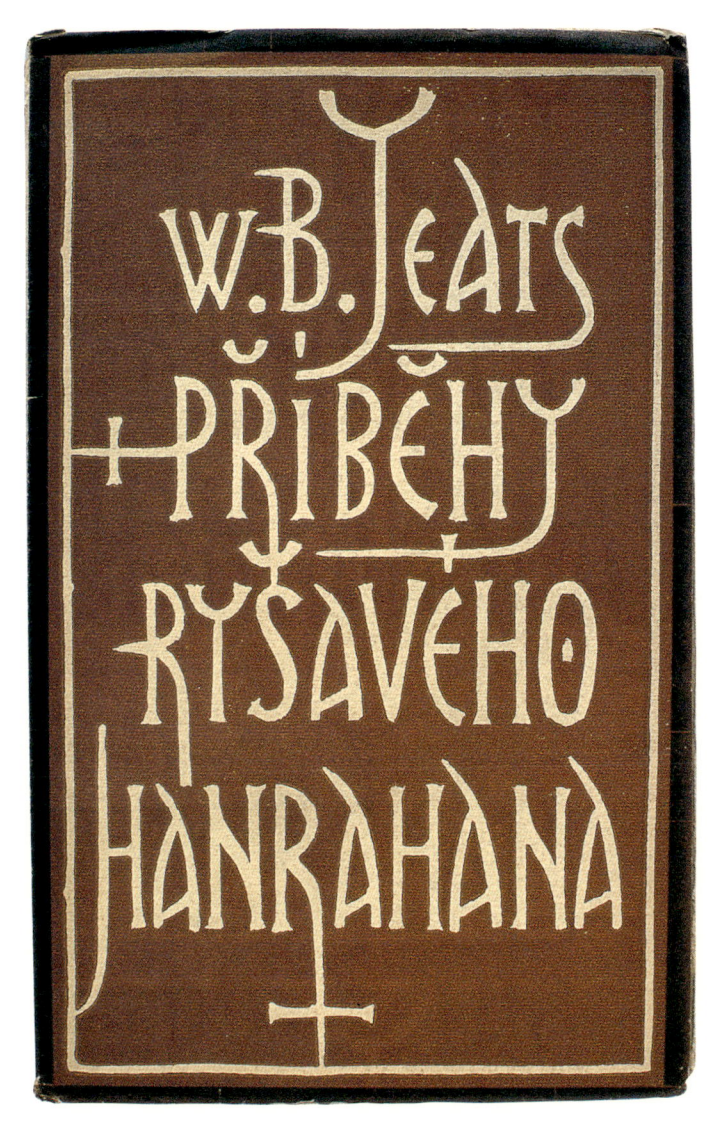

Příběhy ryšavého Hanrahana / W. B. Yeats
Stories of Red Hanrahan / W. B. Yeats
赤毛のハンラハン物語 / ウイリアム・バトラー・イェーツ
1st ed. / 初版
1926

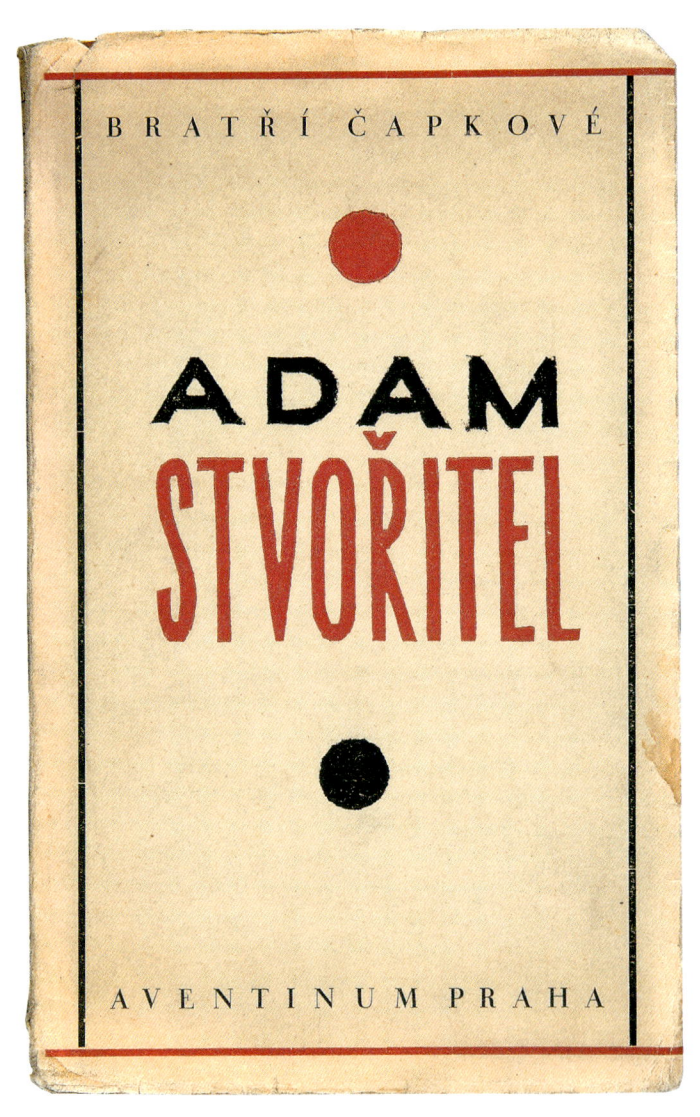

Adam Stvořitel / Bratří Čapkové
Adam the Creator / Josef & Karel Čapek
創造者アダム / チャペック兄弟
3rd ed. / 3版
1927

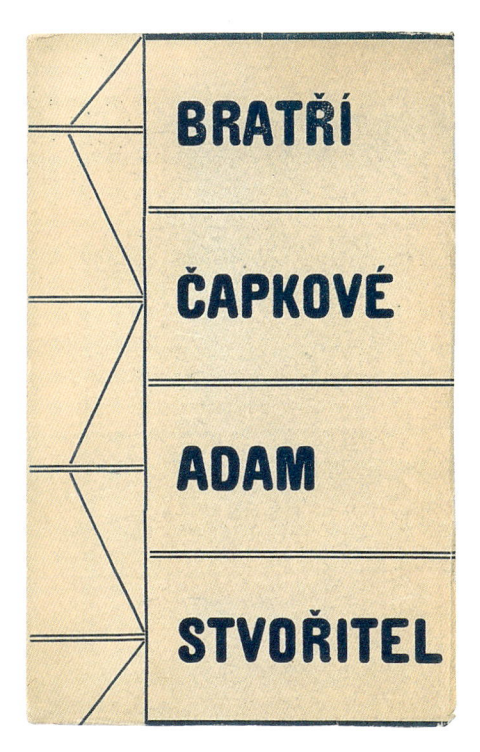

Adam Stvořitel / Bratří Čapkové
Adam the Creator / Josef & Karel Čapek
創造者アダム / チャペック兄弟
5th ed. / 5版
1928

144

Hry s lidmi i věcmi / Josef Kopta
Game with People and Things / Josef Kopta
人や物との遊び / ヨゼフ・コプタ
1st ed. / 初版
1927

145

Grand hotel Nevada / František Langer
Grand Hotel Nevada / František Langer
ネヴァダ・グランドホテル / フランチシェク・ラングル
1st ed. / 初版
1927

146

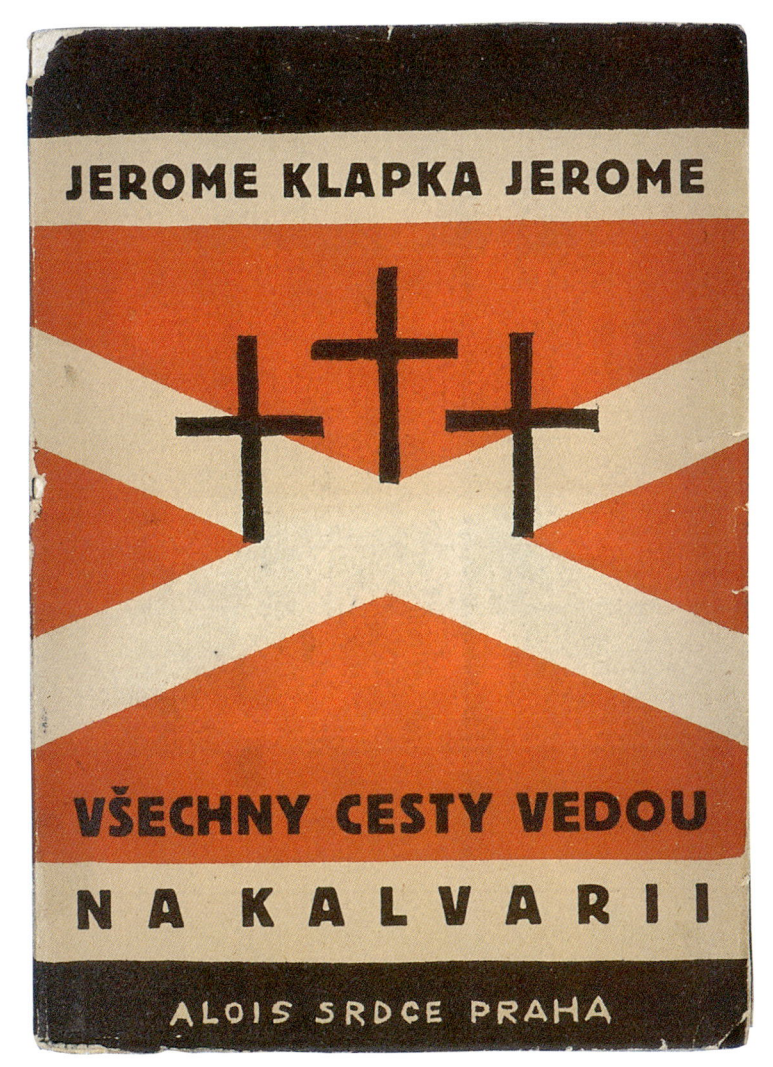

Všechny cesty vedou na Kalvarii / Jerome K. Jerome
All Roads Lead to Calvary / Jerome K. Jerome
すべての道はカルヴァリ(ゴルゴダの丘)に通ず / ジェローム・クラプカ・ジェローム
1st ed. / 初版
1927

148

Putování na dluh / A. C. Nor
Wandering on Credit / A. C. Nor
無銭放浪 / A. C. ノル
1st ed. / 初版
1927

Okolo nás / Karel Poláček
Around Us / Karel Poláček
我々の周辺 / カレル・ポラーチェク
1st ed. / 初版
1927

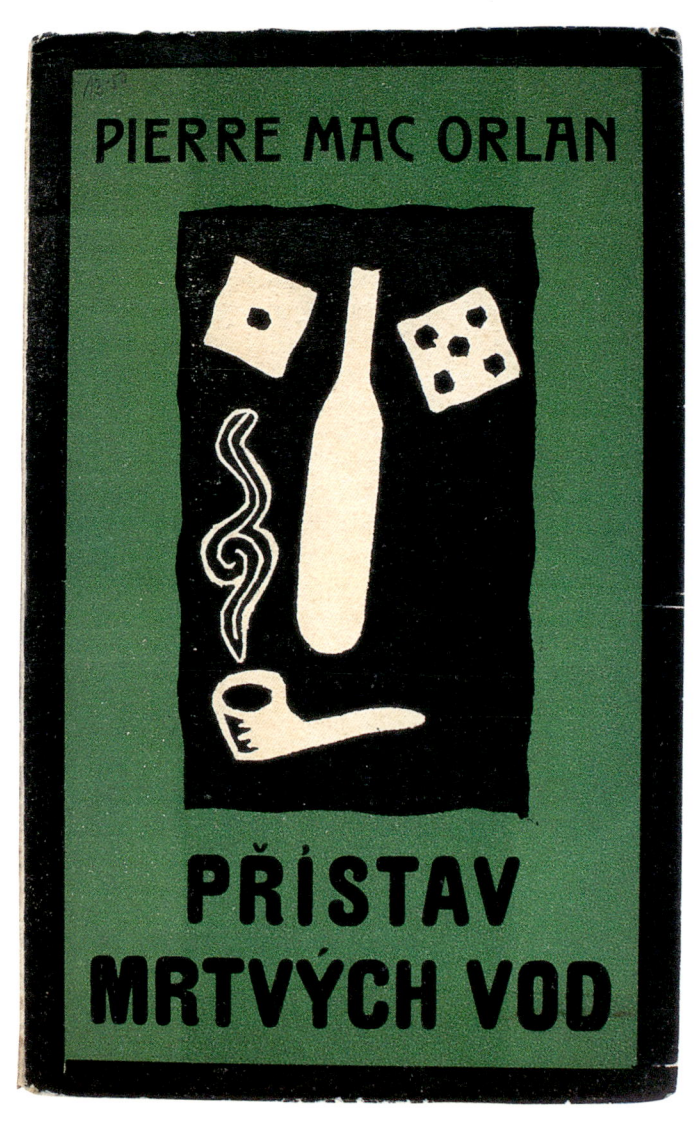

Přístav mrtvých vod / Pierre Mac Orlan
Port of Dead Water / Pierre Mac Orlan
よどんだ水の港 / ピエール・マッコルラン
1st ed. / 初版
1927

151

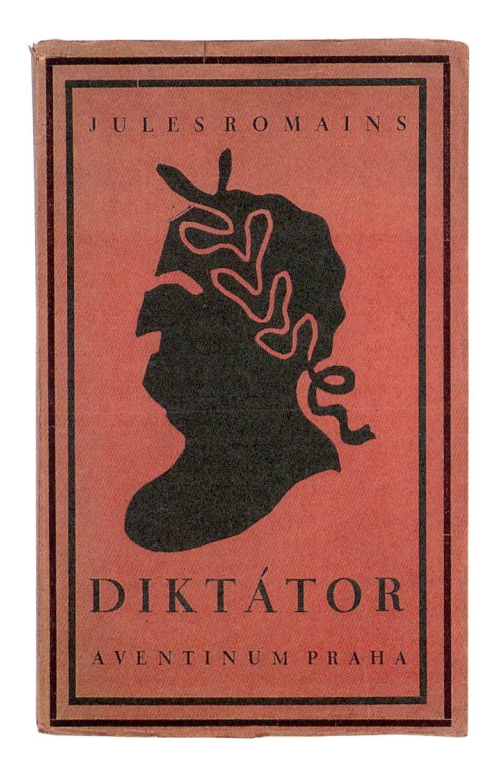

95

Diktátor / Jules Romains
The Dictator / Jules Romains
独裁者 / ジュール・ロマン
1st ed. / 初版
1927

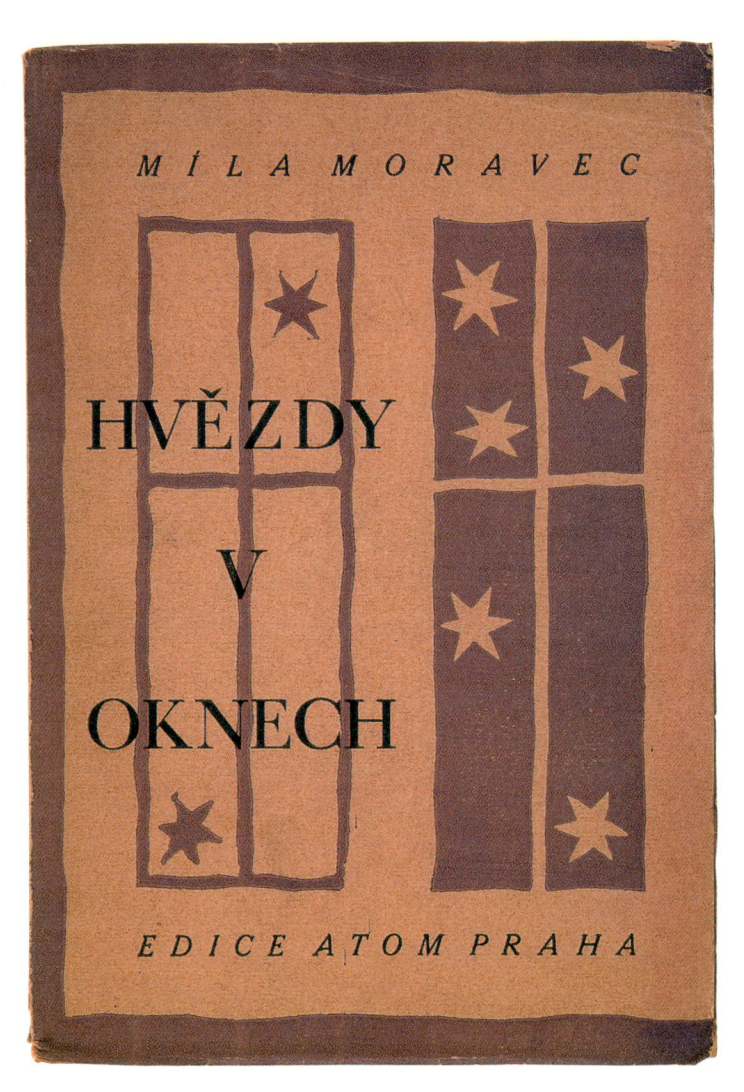

Hvězdy v oknech / Míra Moravec
Stars in the Window / Mira Moravec
窓の中の星 / ミーラ・モラヴェツ
1st ed. / 初版
1927

153

154

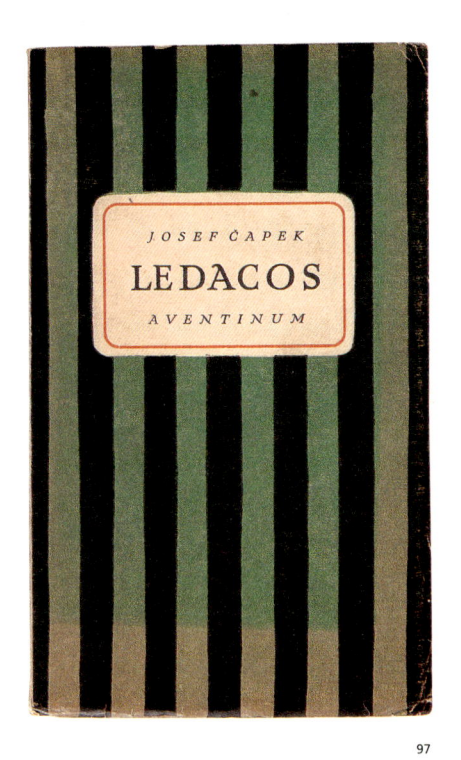

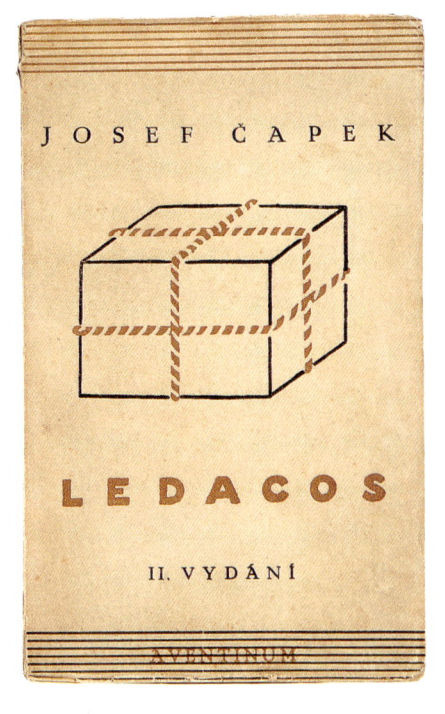

Ledacos / Josef Čapek
All Sorts of Things / Josef Čapek
あれやこれや / ヨゼフ・チャペック
1st ed. / 初版
1928

Ledacos / Josef Čapek
All Sorts of Things / Josef Čapek
あれやこれや / ヨゼフ・チャペック
2nd ed. / 2版
1929

155

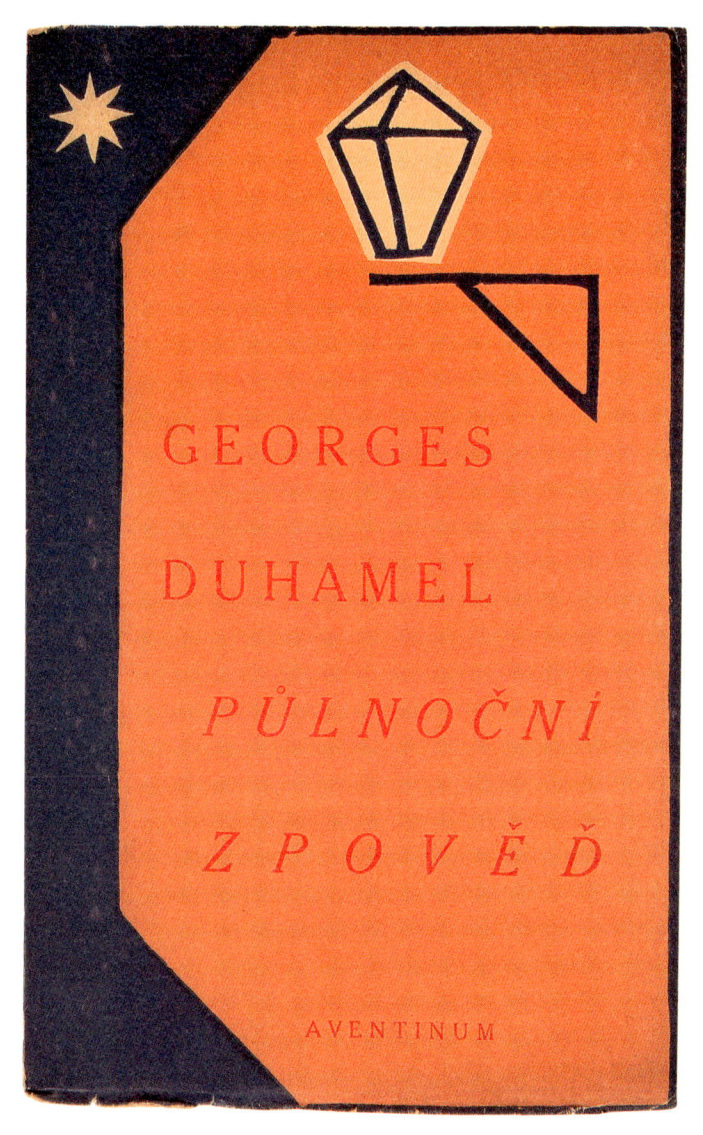

Půlnoční zpověď / Georges Duhamel
Midnight Confession / Georges Duhamel
深夜の告白 / ジョルジュ・デュアメル
1st ed. / 初版
1928

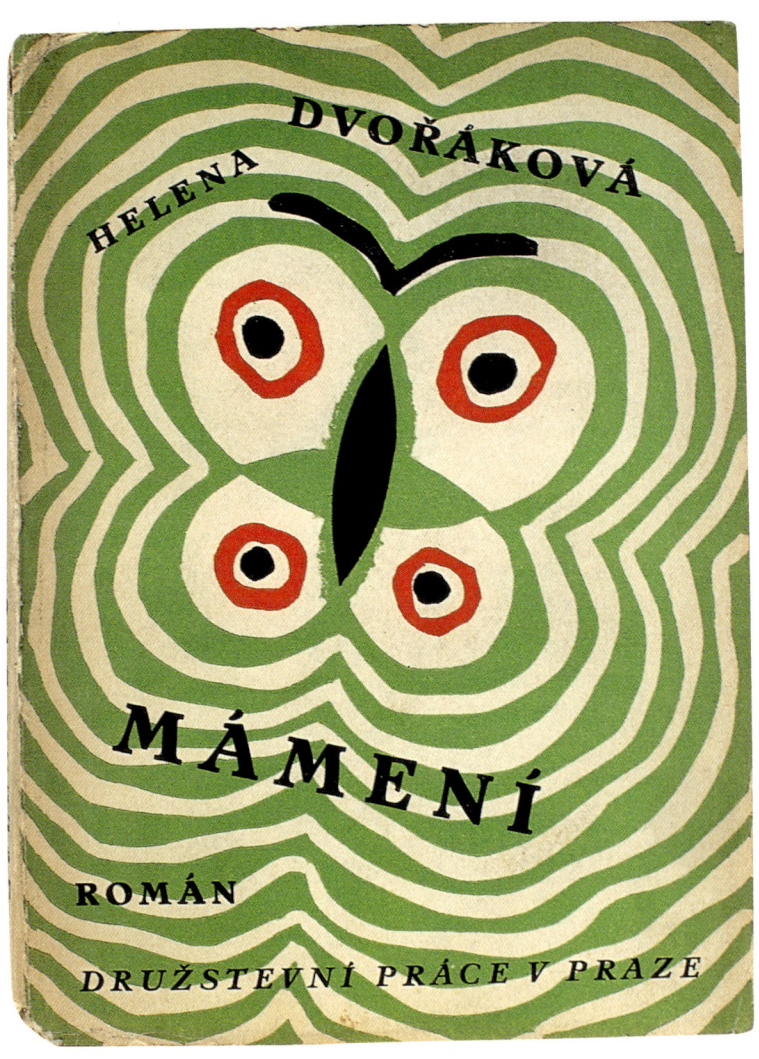

Mámení / Helena Dvořáková
Delusions / Helena Dvořáková
妄想 / ヘレナ・ドヴォジャーコヴァー
6th ed. / 6版
1928

BARVY

Muž který chtěl ABCDE

Tale of a man who wanted to:
A=To do good, B=To hold his own wedding, C=To make his wife happy,
D=To have children, any children, E=To cure influenza

A: 善行をする。B: 自分の結婚式を行う。C: 自分の妻を幸福にする。
D: どんな子でもいいから子供を持つ。E: インフルエンザを治す…ことを望んだ男の物語。

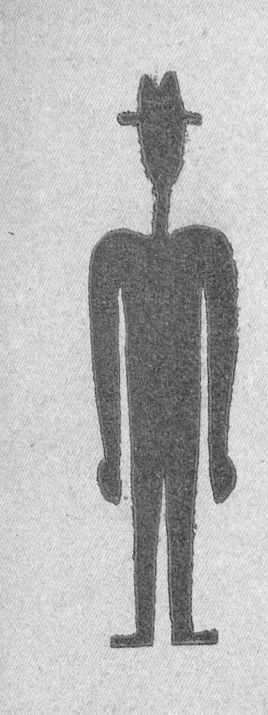

BENJAMIN
KLIČKA

MUŽ A B
KTERÝ C
CHTĚL D E

DRUŽSTEVNÍ PRÁCE PRAHA

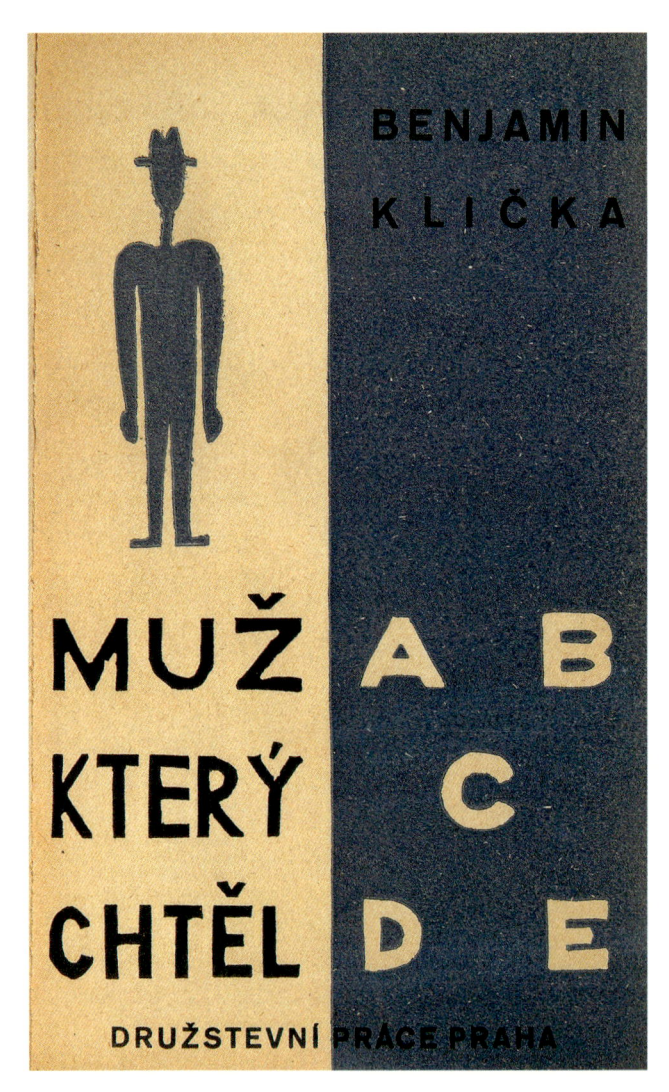

Muž který chtěl ABCDE / Benjamin Klička
The Man Who Desired ABCDE / Benjamin Klička
ABCDEを欲しがった男 / ベンジャミン・クリチカ
1st ed. / 初版
1928

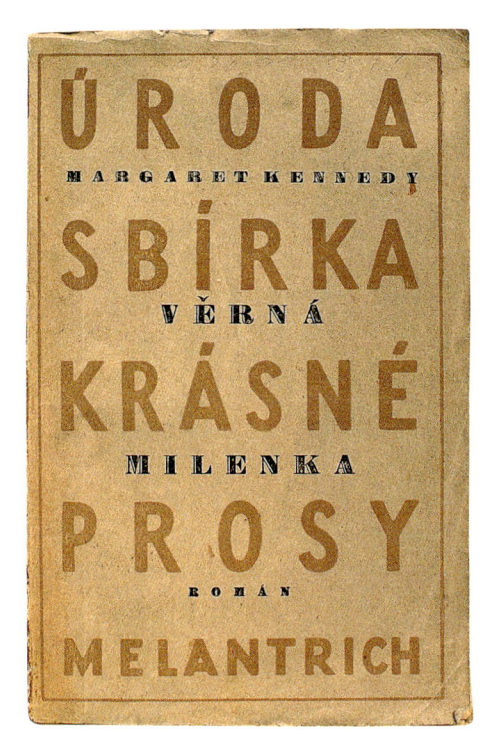

Věrná milenka / Margaret Kennedy
The Constant Nymph / Margaret Kennedy
誠実な恋人 / マーガレット・ケネディ
1st ed. / 初版
1928

Pestré osmero / Benjamin Klička
Eight Multi-coloured Pieces / Benjamin Klička
色とりどりの8篇 / ベンジャミン・クリチカ
1st ed. / 初版
1928

Olbřím / Edmond Konrád
Colossus / Edmond Konrád
巨像 / エドモント・コンラート
1st ed. / 初版
1928

164

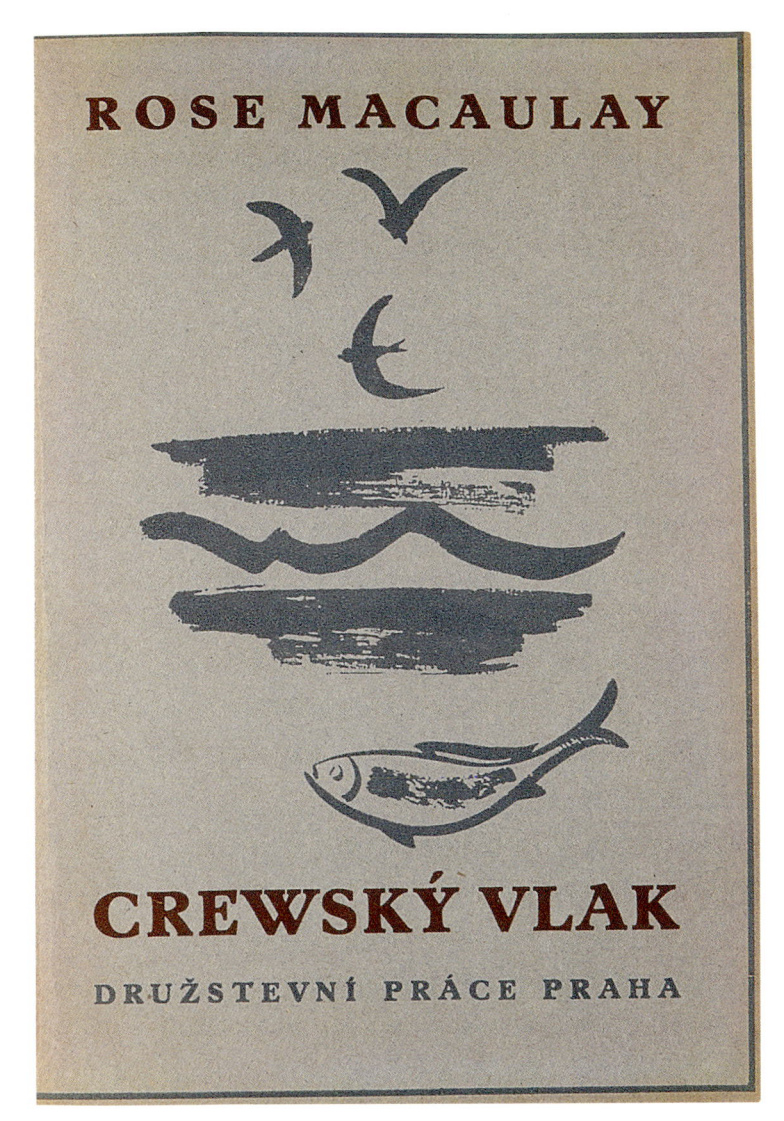

Crewský vlak / Rose Macaulay
Crewe Train / Rose Macaulay
クルーの列車 / ローズ・マコーレイ
1st ed. / 初版
1929

Náměstí republiky / Marie Majerová
Republic Square / Marie Majerová
共和国広場 / マリエ・マイエロヴァー
1st ed. / 初版
1929

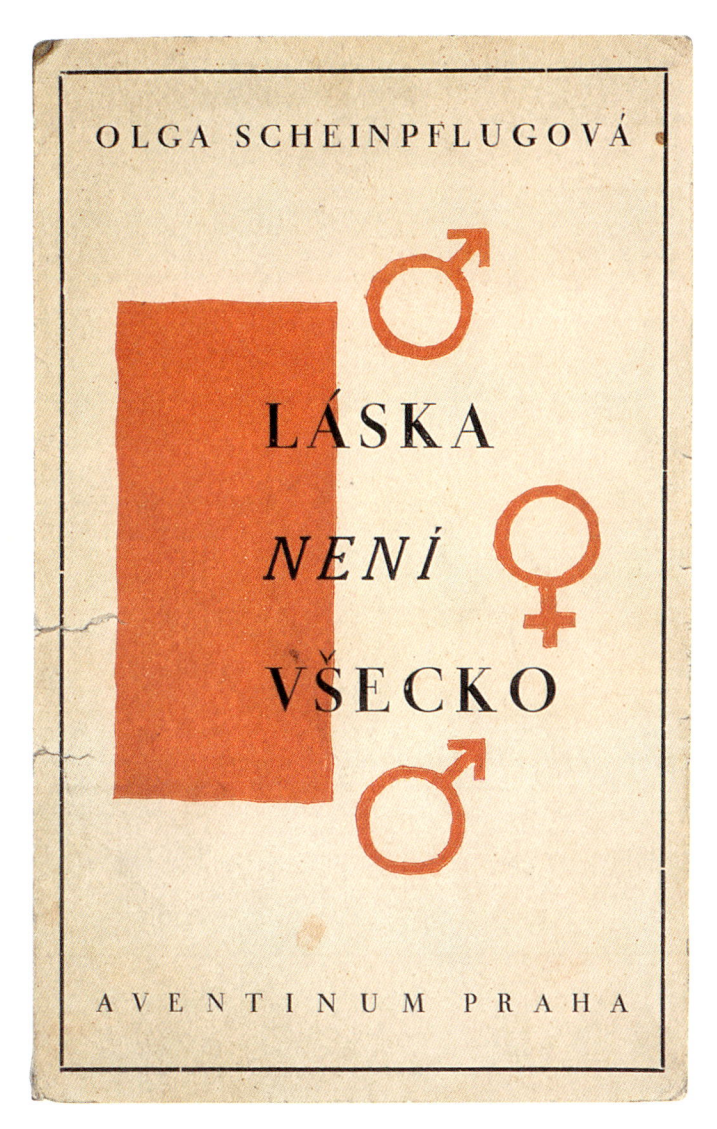

Láska není všecko / Olga Scheinpflugová
Love Isn't Everything / Olga Scheinpflugová
愛がすべてではない / オルガ・シャインフルゴヴァー
2nd ed. / 2版
1929

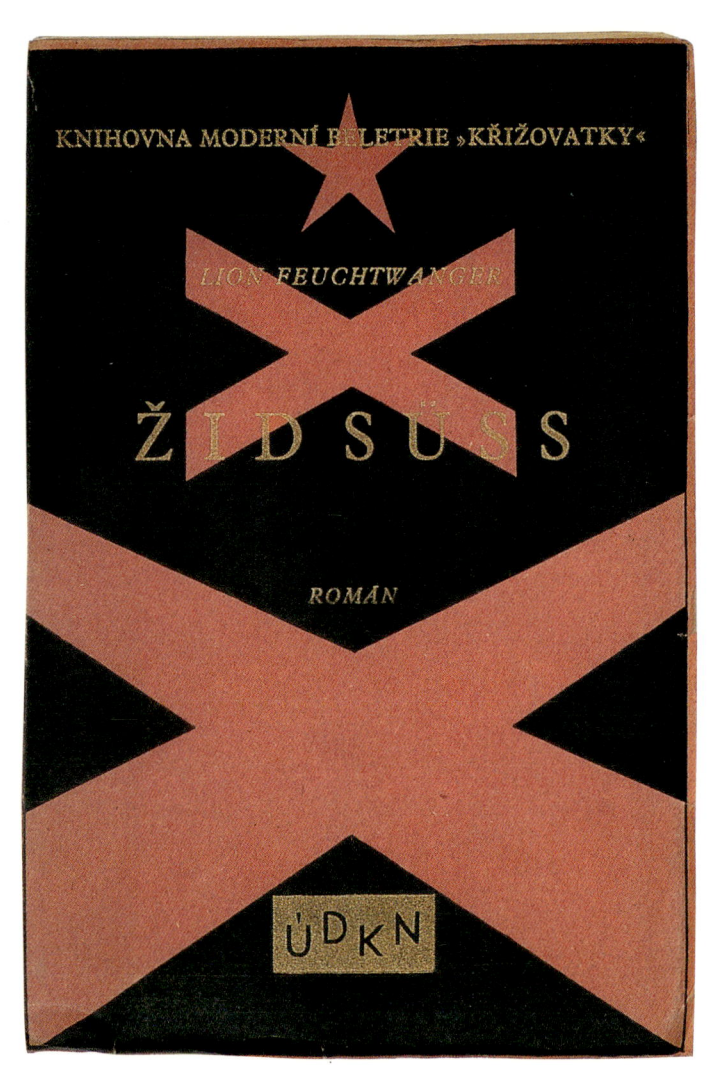

Žid Süss / Lion Feuchtwanger
The Jew Süss / Lion Feuchtwanger
ユダヤ人ジュース / リオン・フォイヒトヴァンガー
Edition unknown / 版不明
1929

169

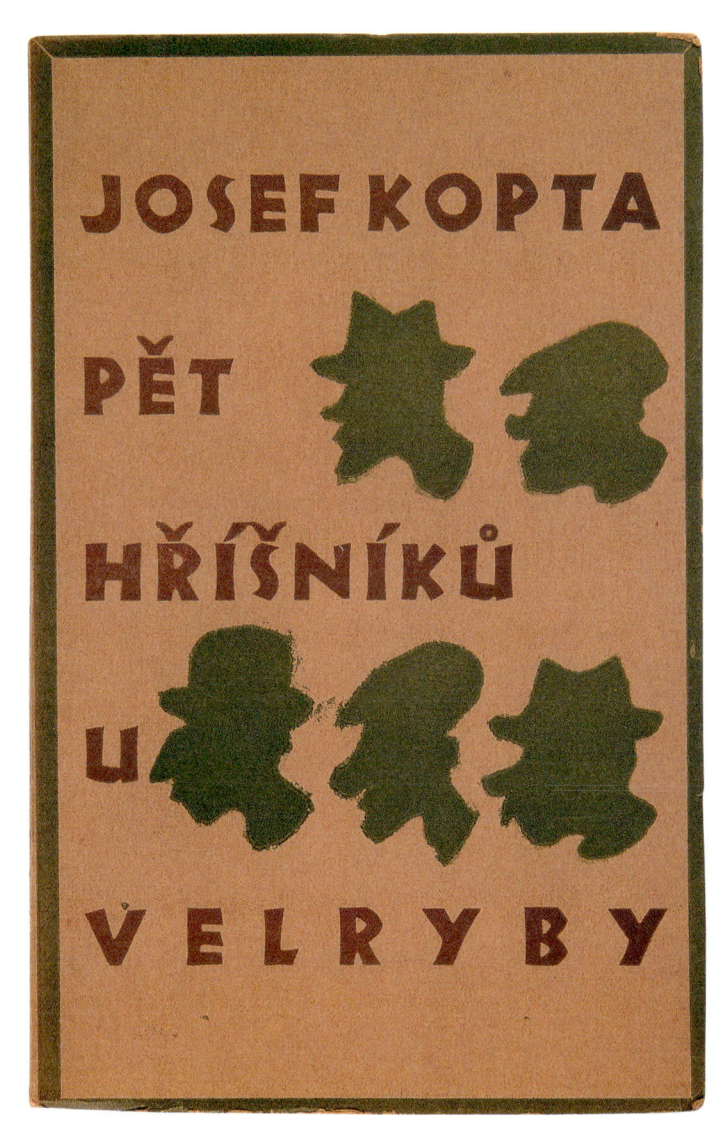

Pět Hříšníků u velryby / Josef Kopta
Five Sinners by a Whale / Josef Kopta
くじらのもとの5人の罪人 / ヨゼフ・コプタ
4th ed. / 4版
1930

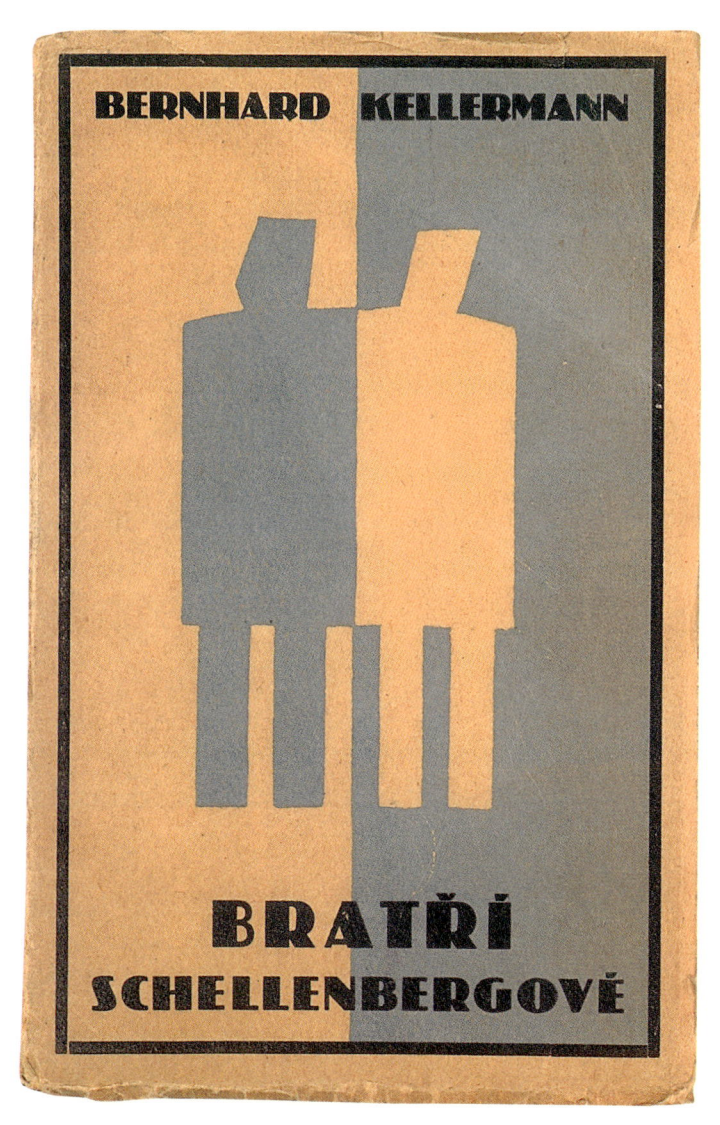

Bratři Schellenbergové / Bernhard Kellermann
The Schellenberg Brothers / Bernhard Kellermann
シェレンベルク兄弟 / ベルンハルト・ケラーマン
3rd ed. / 3版
1930

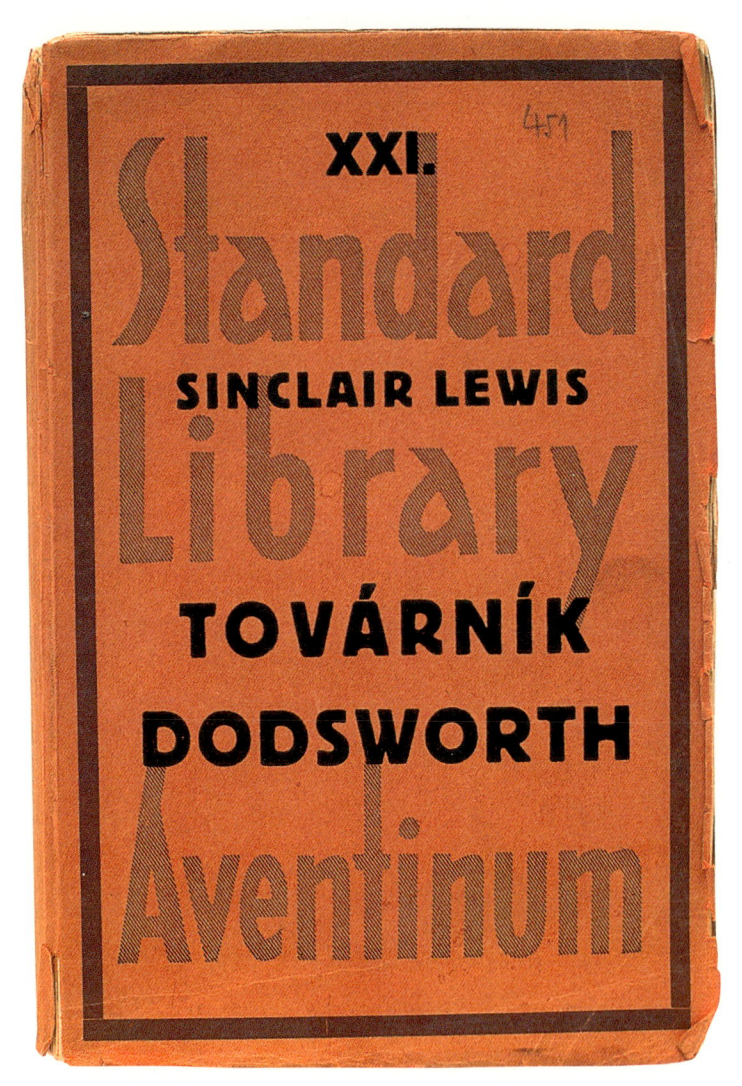

Továrník Dodsworth / Sinclair Lewis
Dodsworth / Sinclair Lewis
工場主、ドッズワース / シンクレア・ルイス
1st ed. / 初版
1931

173

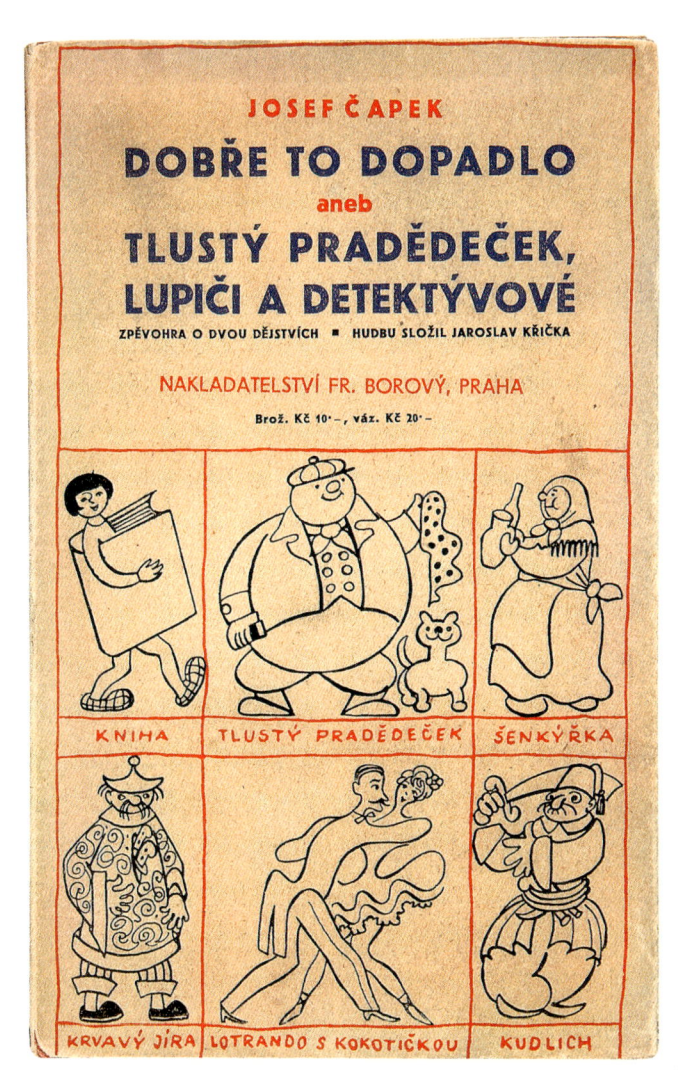

Dobře to dopadlo aneb Tlustý pradědeček, lupiči a detektývové / Josef Čapek
'All's Well That Ends Well, Or The Fat Great-Granddad, the Thief and the Detectives' / Josef Čapek
うまくいった、あるいは太ったひいおじいさんと泥棒と探偵たち / ヨゼフ・チャペック
1st ed. / 初版
1932

174

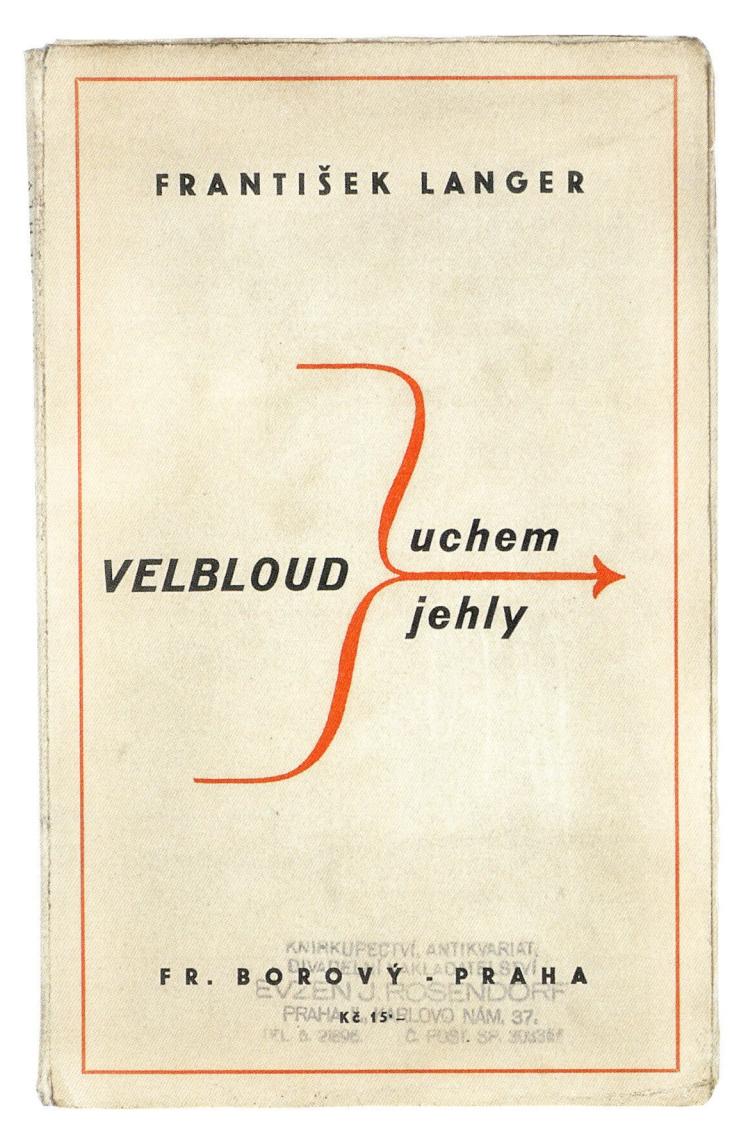

Velbloud uchem jehly / František Langer
A Camel through the Eye of a Needle / František Langer
針の目を通ったラクダ / フランチシェク・ラングル
1st ed. / 初版
1934

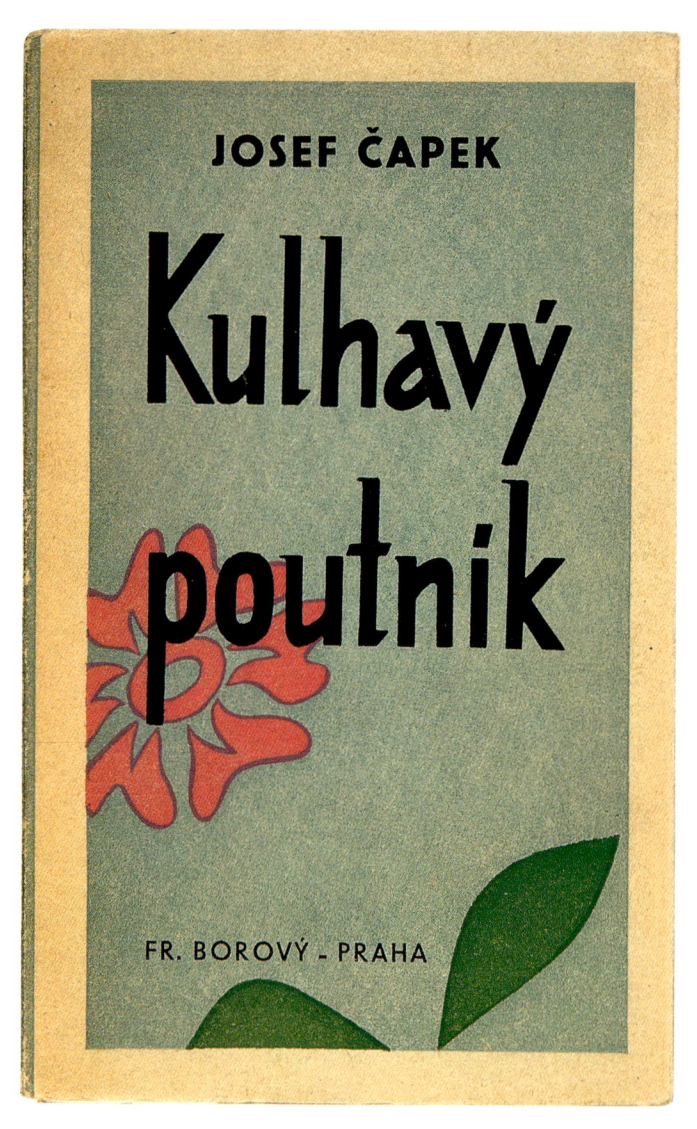

Kulhavý poutnik (Co jsem na světě uviděl) / Josef Čapek
Limping Wanderer (What I Saw in the World) / Josef Čapek
片足をひきずって歩く放浪者（私が世界で何を見たか）/ ヨゼフ・チャペック
4th ed. / 4版
1937

177

Továrna na absolutno

Fiction. An engineer advertises his invention in a newspaper,
 and his former school mate, a company president, comes to call.
The invention is atomic energy that uses up matter 100%.
The engineer explains that after all matter is used up,
the 'absolute' will remain, a pure god.
The company grows through this invention but with nowhere to go,
the 'absolute' runs the factory at will and begins to control society.
The absolute becomes 'god' and the various ethnic groups with their different gods
begin conflicts which grow into a major war.

マレックという技師が自分の発明を買ってくれるよう新聞広告を出す。
それを見た昔の同級生で、MEASという会社の社長であるボンディ氏がマレックを訪ねる。
発明とは物質を100％使いきる原子エネルギーだった。
マレックはボンディ氏に物質が完全に失われると後に「絶対」が残る、純粋の神が残る、と説明する。
ボンディ氏の会社はその発明によって発展するが、
行き所を無くした「絶対」がかってに工場を動かしだし、社会を支配し始める。
「絶対」は神となり、各々の神を持った民族はお互いに争い始め、大きな戦争へと発展する。

KAREL ČAPEK

TOVÁRNA
NA ABSOLUTNO

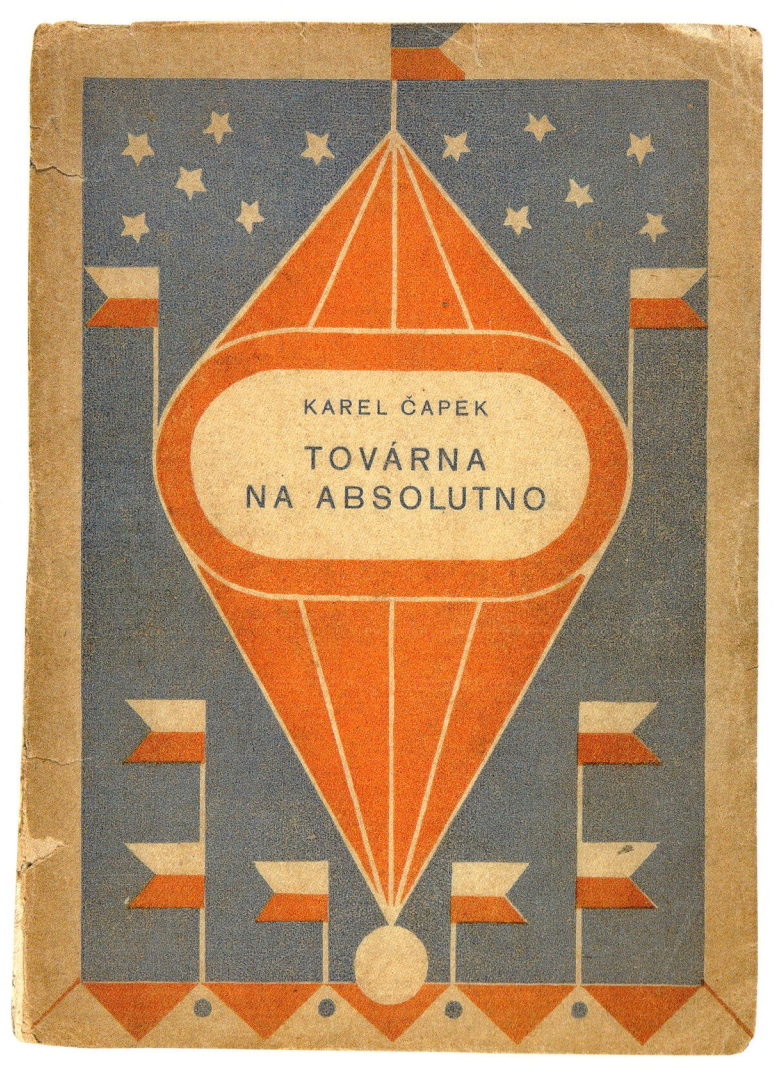

Továrna na absolutno / Karel Čapek
The Absolute at Large / Karel Čapek
絶対子工場 / カレル・チャペック
1st ed. / 初版
1922

181

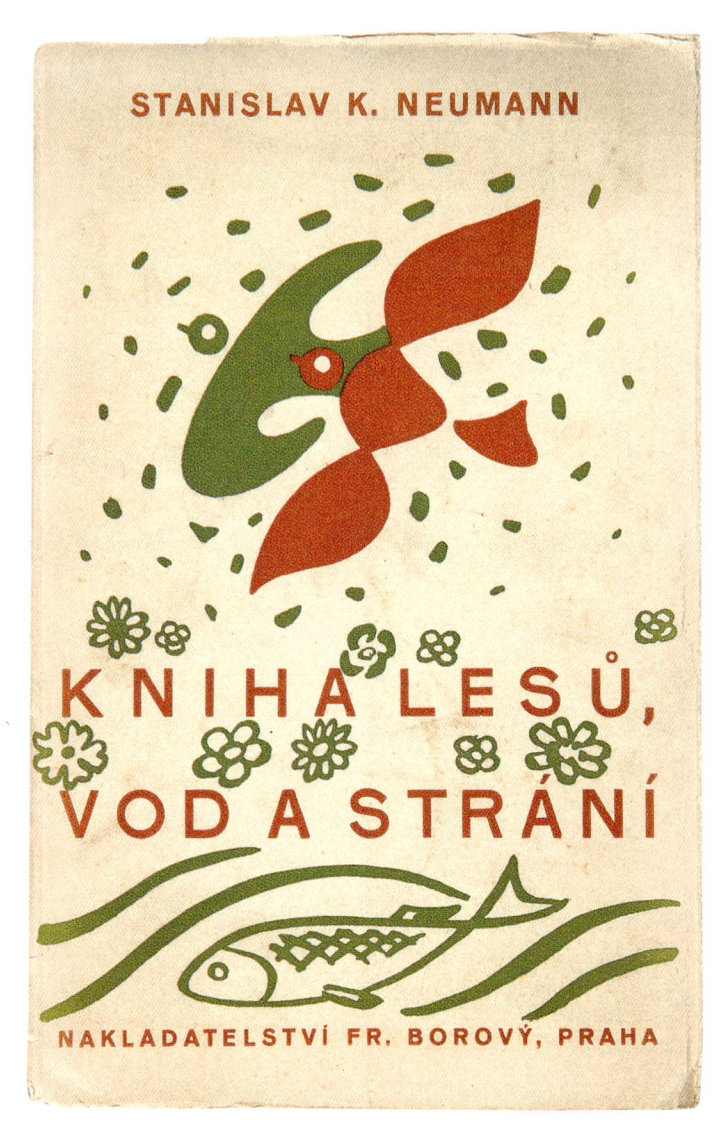

Kniha lesů, vod a strání / Stanislav Kostka Neumann
The Book of Woodland, Water and Hillsides / Stanislav Kostka Neumann
森と水と山腹の本 / スタニスラフ・コストカ・ノイマン
3rd ed. / 3版
1938

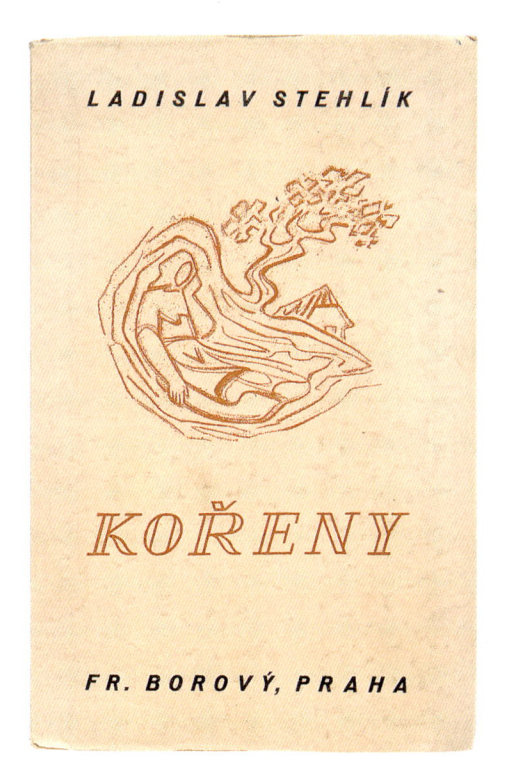

Kořeny / Ladislav Stehlík
Roots / Ladislav Stehlík
根 / ラジスラフ・ステフリーク
1st ed. / 初版
1938

184

185

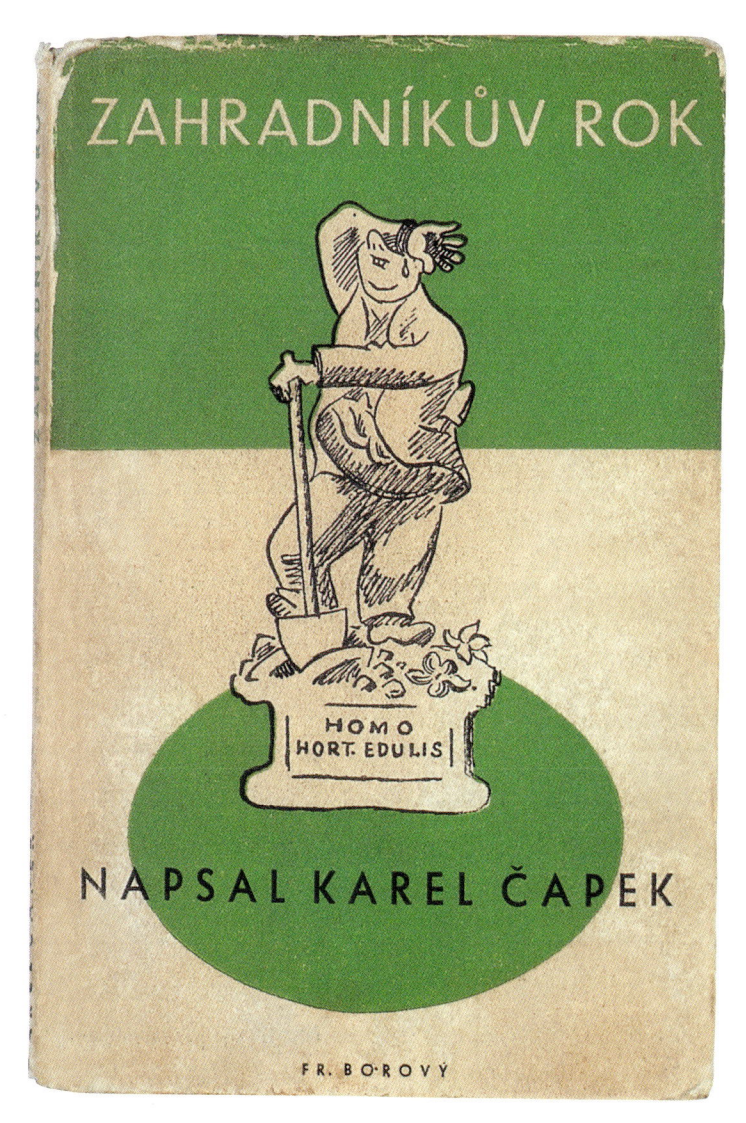

Zahradníkův rok / Karel Čapek
The Gardener's Year / Karel Čapek
園芸家12ヵ月 / カレル・チャペック
Edition unknown / 版不明
1947

Bidýlko / Emil Vachek
Perch / Emil Vachek
とまり木 / エミル・ヴァヘック
1st ed. from Czechoslovakian Writers Press / 12版（チェコスロバキア作家出版として初版）
1954

187

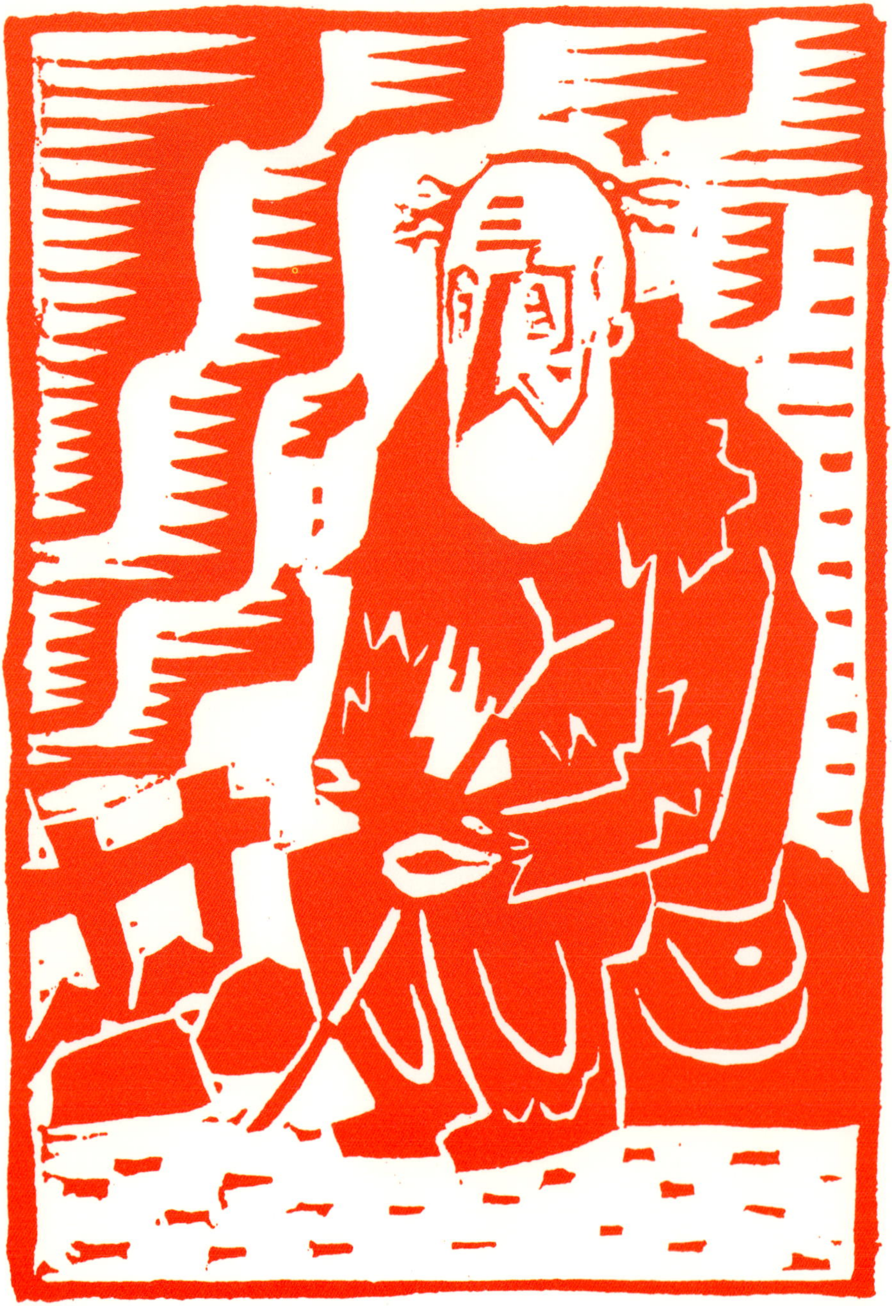

作品リスト／List of Works

055

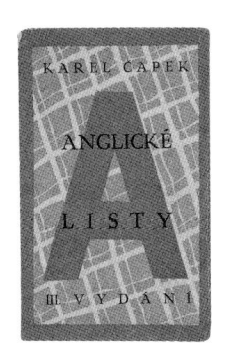

Anglické listy / Karel Čapek
Lady into Fox / Karel Čapek
キツネになった貴婦人 / デビッド・ガーネット
1925 / 3rd ed. 3版 / 198mm×125mm
1996 / 恒文社

Karel Čapek's experiences in England, particularly London, and Scotland. With numerous illustrations by the author.

カレル・チャペックのイギリス旅行記。ロンドンを中心に英国と、スコットランドでの体験記。カレルの手によるイラストが多数含まれる。

- ●作品番号　Reference number
- ●タイトル / 著者（チェコ語）　Title / author in Czech
- ●タイトル / 著者（英語）　Title / author in English
- ●タイトル / 著者（日本語）　Title / author in Japanese
- ●出版年 / 重版 / サイズ　Publication date / edition / Size
- ●日本での出版歴　出版年 / 出版社　Publication in Japan / date / publisher
- ●Genre, synopsis, etc.
- ●本のジャンル、あらすじなど

※英語・日本語タイトルについて
すでに英語・日本語で出版された「定訳」があるものについてはそれを記しました。
ないものに関しては、チェコ語から直訳したものを載せています。
※日本での出版歴
出版社名は主なものを載せました。
記載されていない出版社からも出版されている可能性があります。

Book titles in English, Japanese:
Where a translation into English or Japanese has been published,
the published title is given.
Titles of works with no known published translations
have been directly translated from the Czech.
Publication in Japan:
Main publisher's name is given.
 (Some works may have been published by more than one publisher).

001

Nejskromnější umění / Josef Čapek
The Most Modest Art / Josef Čapek
最も謙虚な芸術 / ヨゼフ・チャペック
1920 / 1st ed. 初版 / 145mm×215mm

Seven chapters on simple folk art
素朴な民間芸術に関する7章

002

Francouzská poesie nové doby / Karel Čapek
New Era French Poetry / Karel Čapek
新時代のフランス詩 / カレル・チャペック
1920 / 1st ed. 初版 / 175mm×135mm

Karel's translations of the work of French poets
フランスの詩人による詩のカレルによるチェコ語訳

003

Kritika slov / Karel Čapek
A Critique of Words / Karel Čapek
言葉の批評 / カレル・チャペック
1920 / 1st ed. 初版 / 143mm×94mm

Short commentary on 52 words such as 'death', 'proverb' and 'truth'
「死」「諺」「真実」など52の言葉に対して短いコメントをしている

004

Kritika slov / Karel Čapek
A Critique of Words / Karel Čapek
言葉の批評 / カレル・チャペック
1927 / 2nd ed. 2版 / 202mm×124mm

Short commentary on 52 words such as 'death', 'proverb' and 'truth'
「死」「諺」「真実」など52の言葉に対して短いコメントをしている

005

Loupežník / Karel Čapek
The Robber / Karel Čapek
盗人 / カレル・チャペック
1920 / 1st ed. 初版 / 220mm×151mm

See P22 / P22 参照

006

Mladým lidem / Petr Kropotkin
An Appeal to the Young / Petr Kropotkin
若い人々へ / ピョートル・クロポトキン
1920 / 1st ed. 初版 / 177mm×111mm

Containing two collections of reviews: 'An Appeal To The Young', '100Years On Standby' Translated by Junius

「若い人々へ」と「100年の待機」の2編の評論を収録
ユニウス訳

007

Malé děvče / Helena Čapková
The Small Girl / Helena Čapková
小さな少女 / ヘレナ・チャプコヴァー
1920 / 1st ed. 初版 / 172mm×131mm

Novel authored by Čapek brothers older sister Helena.

チャペック兄弟の姉のヘレナが書いた小説

008

R.U.R. (Rossum's Universal Robots) / Karel Čapek
R.U.R. (Rossum's Universal Robots) / Karel Čapek
R.U.R.（ロッスムのユニバーサルロボット）/ カレル・チャペック
1920 / 1st ed. 初版 / 223mm×152mm
1989 / 岩波書店 他

See P26 / P26 参照

009

R.U.R. (Rossum's Universal Robots) / Karel Čapek
R.U.R. (Rossum's Universal Robots) / Karel Čapek
R.U.R.（ロッスムのユニバーサルロボット）/ カレル・チャペック
1921 / 2nd ed. 2版 / 215mm×137mm
1989 / 岩波書店 他

See P26 / P26 参照

010

R.U.R. (Rossum's Universal Robots) / Karel Čapek
R.U.R. (Rossum's Universal Robots) / Karel Čapek
R.U.R.（ロッスムのユニバーサルロボット）/ カレル・チャペック
1922 / 4th ed. 4版 / 218mm×145mm
1989 / 岩波書店 他

See P26 / P26 参照

011

R.U.R. (Rossum's Universal Robots) / Karel Čapek
R.U.R. (Rossum's Universal Robots) / Karel Čapek
R.U.R.（ロッスムのユニバーサルロボット）/ カレル・チャペック
1924 / 6th ed. 6版 / 215mm×145mm
1989 / 岩波書店 他

See P26 / P26 参照

012

Povidky z městského sadu / Marie Pujmanová - Hennerová
Tales from the City Orchard / Marie Pujmanová - Hennerová
市街地の果樹園の物語 / マリエ・プイマノヴァ－ヘネロヴァー
1920 / 1st ed. 初版 / 174mm×110mm

Short stories

短編集

013

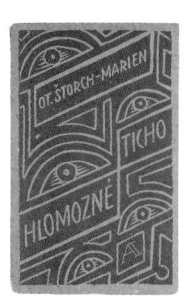

Hlomozné ticho / Otakar Štorch - Marien
Noisy Silence / Otakar Štorch - Marien
騒がしい静寂 / オタカル・シュトルフ－マリエン
1920 / 1st ed. 初版 / 214mm×176mm

Short stories from 1919-20
1919 - 20年の短編集

014

Mistr Petr Pleticha / anonymus
Maître Pierre Patelin (Master Peter Patelin) / Author unknown
マスター・ペトル・プレチハ（ピエール・パトラン）/ 作者不詳
1921 / 1st ed. 初版 / 162mm×122mm

Ancient French comedy. Translated by N. Havel
不明の作家による古代フランスの笑劇　N.ハヴェル訳

015

Trapné povídky / Karel Čapek
Embarrassing Short Stories / Karel Čapek
苦悩に満ちた物語 / カレル・チャペック
1921 / 1st ed. 初版 / 175mm×110mm
1996 / 成文社

Short stories
短い短編集

016

Trapné povídky / Karel Čapek
Embarrassing Short Stories / Karel Čapek
苦悩に満ちた物語 / カレル・チャペック
1926 / 2nd ed. 第2版 / 209mm×143mm
1996 / 成文社

Short stories
短編集

017

Světlo / Georges Duhamel
La Lumiere (Light) / Georges Duhamel
光 / ジョルジュ・デュアメル
1921 / 1st ed. 初版 / 216mm×132mm

Four-act play. Translated by J. Hrdimová
4幕の戯曲 J.フルジノヴァー訳

018

Pokušení svatého Antonína / Gustav Flaubert
La Tentation de Saint Antoine (The Temptation of Saint Anthony) / Gustav Flaubert
聖アントワーヌの誘惑 / ギュスターヴ・フロベール
1921 / 1st ed. 初版 / 198mm×145mm

Translated by J. Borecky
J.ボレツキー訳

019

Hudba na náměstí / Jindřich Hořejší
Music in the Square / Jindřich Hořejší
広場の音楽 / インドジフ・ホジェイシー
1921 / 1st ed. 初版 / 217mm×142mm

Poetry

詩集

020

Zelené demonstrace / František Němec
Demonstration / František Němec
緑色の表明 / フランチシェク・ニェメツ
1921 / 1st ed. 初版 / 212mm×133mm

Poetry

詩集

021

Sen o zástupu zoufajících / Stanislav Kostka Neumann
Dreams of Despairing People / Stanislav Kostka Neumann
絶望する人々についての夢 / スタニスラフ・コストカ・ノイマン
1921 / 1st ed. 初版 / 242mm×197mm

Poetry

詩集

022

Krvavá ironie / Rachilde
Blood Irony / Rachilde
血に染まった皮肉 / ラシルド
1921 / 1st ed. 初版 / 217mm×135mm

Fiction translated by E.Ruttovà
小説　E.ルトヴァー訳

023

Věc Makropulos / Karel Čapek
The Makropulos Secret / Karel Čapek
マクロプロス事件 / カレル・チャペック
1922 / 2nd ed. 2版 / 215mm×145mm
1998 / 八月舎

See P42 / P42参照

024

Věc Makropulos / Karel Čapek
The Makropulos Secret / Karel Čapek
マクロプロス事件 / カレル・チャペック
1923 / 3rd ed. 3版 / 214mm×145mm

See P42 / P42参照

025

Kolébka / Helena Čapková
Cradle / Helena Čapková
揺りかご / ヘレナ・チャプコヴァー
1922 / 1st ed. 初版 / 175mm×132mm

Fiction

小説

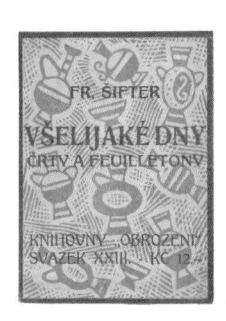

026

Všelijaké dny / František Šifter
All Sorts of Days / Frantisek Sifter
あらゆる日々 / フランチシェク・シフテル
1922 / 1st ed. 初版 / 193mm×142mm

Essays

エッセイ集

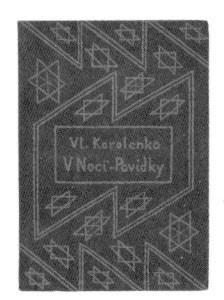

027

V noci / Vladimír Korolenko
At Night / Vladimir Korolenko
夜に / ウラジーミル・コロレンコ
1922 / 1st ed. 初版 / 197mm×143mm

Five short stories translated by Fr. Šifter

5編の短編集　Fr.シフテル訳

028

Ze života hmyzu / Bratří Čapkové
The Life of the Insects / Josef & Karel Čapek
虫の生活 / チャペック兄弟
1922 / 3rd ed. 3版 / 209mm×130mm
1925 / 原始社

See P50 / P50 参照

029

Ze života hmyzu / Bratří Čapkové
The Life of the Insects / Josef & Karel Čapek
虫の生活 / チャペック兄弟
1922 / 2nd ed. 2版 / 215mm×137mm
1925 / 原始社

See P50 / P50 参照

030

Osvobozená slova / Osvobozená slova / F. T. Marinetti
Les Mots en Liberte Futuristes (Manifesto of Futurism) / F. T. Marinetti
解放された言葉 / F. T. マリネッティ
1922 / 2nd ed. 2版 / 205mm×136mm

Translated by Macák

J.マツァーク訳

031

Soudy, boje a výzvy let 1920-22 / A. M. Píša
Judgements, Struggles and Appeals of the Years 1920-22 / A. M. Píša
1920-22年の判決、戦い、そして訴え / A. M. ピーシャ
1922 / 1st ed. 初版 / 192mm×142mm

Criticism

評論集

032

Lásky hra osudná / Bratří Čapkové
Love's Fateful Game / Josef & Karel Čapek
愛の運命のいたずら / チャペック兄弟
1922 / 1st ed. 初版 / 169mm×109mm

One-act play written in 1910

1910年に書かれた1幕劇

033

Pro delfína / Josef Čapek
For the Dolphin / Josef Čapek
イルカのために / ヨゼフ・チャペック
1923 / 1st ed. 初版 / 153mm×92mm

Seven stories written between 1917 and 1923

1917-23年に書かれた7つの短編を集めたもの

034

Lelio a Pro delfína / Josef Čapek
Lelio & For the Dolphin / Josef Čapek
レーリオとイルカのために / ヨゼフ・チャペック
1925 / 2nd ed. 2版 / 203mm×144mm

Short stories
短編集

035

Málo o mnohém / Josef Čapek
A Little about a Lot of Things / Josef Čapek
たくさんのことについて少し / ヨゼフ・チャペック
1923 / 1st ed. 初版 / 212mm×150mm

His thoughts on art and taste.
芸術とセンスに関しての考えを述べている

036

Země mnoha jmen / Josef Čapek
The Country with Many Names / Josef Čapek
たくさんの名前を持つ国 / ヨゼフ・チャペック
1923 / 1st ed. 初版 / 214mm×140mm

Play in three acts and one scene
3幕と1場の戯曲

037

Země mnoha jmen / Josef Čapek
The Country with Many Names / Josef Čapek
たくさんの名前を持つ国 / ヨゼフ・チャペック
1923 / 2nd ed. 2版 / 210mm×135mm

Play in three acts and one scene
3幕と1場の戯曲

038

Italské listy / Karel Čapek
Letters from Italy / Karel Čapek
イタリアからの手紙 / カレル・チャペック
1923 / 1st ed. 初版 / 199mm×124mm

See P60 / P60 参照

039

Italské listy / Karel Čapek
Letters from Italy / Karel Čapek
イタリアからの手紙 / カレル・チャペック
1924 / 2nd ed. 2版 / 199mm×124mm

See P60 / P60 参照

040

Italské listy / Karel Čapek
Letters from Italy / Karel Čapek
イタリアからの手紙 / カレル・チャペック
1925 / 3rd ed. 3版 / 200mm×125mm

See P60 / P60 参照

041

Italské listy / Karel Čapek
Letters of Italy / Karel Čapek
イタリアからの手紙 / カレル・チャペック
1926 / 4th ed. 4版 / 199mm×124mm

See P60 / P60 参照

042

Občanská válka / Jiří Haussman
Civil War / Jiří Haussman
市民戦争 / イジー・ハウスマン
1923 / 1st ed. 初版 / 210mm×145mm

Political poetry

政治的な詩集

043

Červen / Fráňa Šrámek
June / Fráňa Šrámek
6月 / フラーニャ・シュラーメック
1923 / 2nd ed. 2版 / 185mm×120mm

One-act play
1幕の戯曲

044

Plačící satyr / Fráňa Šrámek
The Crying Satyr / Fráňa Šrámek
泣いているサテュロス / フラーニャ・シュラーメック
1923 / 1st ed. 初版 / 220mm×150mm

Three-act play
3幕の戯曲

045

Objevy / Charles Vidlrac
Discoveries / Charles Vidlrac
発見 / シャルル・ヴィルドゥラック
1923 / 1st ed. 初版 / 213mm×134mm

Short stories and one-act play translated by Hrdinová
短編集と1幕の戯曲　J.フルジノヴァー訳

046

Boží muka / Karel Čapek
Wayside Column / Karel Čapek
受難像 / カレル・チャペック
1924 / 2nd ed. 2版 / 210mm×150mm
1995 / 成文社

13 short stories

13の短編集

047

Krakatit / Karel Čapek
Krakatit / Karel Čapek
クラカチット / カレル・チャペック
1924 / 1st ed. 初版 / 195mm×149mm
1992 / 楡出版

Science fiction. Tale of a chemical engineer who discovers a material with enormous explosive power.

SF小説 巨大な爆発物を発見した化学技師プロコップをめぐる物語

048

FU / František Kubka
FU / František Kubka
FU / フランチシェク・クブカ
1924 / 1st ed. 初版 / 183mm×123mm

Short stories

短編集

049

Zářivé hlubiny a jiné prosy / Bratří Čapkové
The Shining Depths and Other Stories / Josef & Karel Čapek
輝く深淵と他の物語 / チャペック兄弟
1924 / 2nd ed. 2版 / 205mm×148mm

Short stories
短編集

050

Knížka o českém charakteru / Jiří Mahen
On Czech Characteristics / Jiří Mahen
チェコ的特徴についての本 / イジー・マヘン
1924 / 1st ed. 初版 / 210mm×315mm

Philosophical observations on everyday issues
一般的な問題に対して哲学的な考察をしている

051

Soud / Fráňa Šrámek
The Judgement / Fráňa Šrámek
判決 / フラーニャ・シュラーメック
1924 / 1st ed. 初版 / 213mm×134mm

Three-act play
3幕の戯曲　KOMEDIEとは喜劇のこと

052

Zloděj z Bagdadu / Konstantin Biebl
Thief from Baghdad / Konstantin Biebl
バグダッドの盗賊 / コンスタンチン・ビーブル
1925 / 1st ed. 初版 / 185mm×125mm

Poetry

詩集

053

Měsíční vitriol / Henri Béraud
Le Vitriol de Lune (Vitriol of the Moon) / Henri Béraud
月の硫酸塩 / アンリ・ベロー
1925 / 1st ed. 初版 / 195mm×145mm

Fiction Translated by Mathesius

小説　B.マテジウス訳

054

Anglické listy / Karel Čapek
Letters from England / Karel Čapek
イギリス便り / カレル・チャペック
1925 / 2nd ed. 2版 / 199mm×123mm
1996 / 恒文社　他

See P82 / P82 参照

055

Anglické listy / Karel Čapek
Letters from England / Karel Čapek
イギリス便り / カレル・チャペック
1925 / 3rd ed. 3版 / 198mm×125mm
1996 / 恒文社 他

See P82 / P82 参照

056

Anglické listy / Karel Čapek
Letters from England / Karel Čapek
イギリス便り / カレル・チャペック
1927 / 4th ed. 4版 / 199mm×124mm
1996 / 恒文社 他

See P82 / P82 参照

057

Noc / František Langer
Night / Frantisek Langer
夜 / フランチシェク・ラングル
1925 / 1st ed. 初版 / 254mm×183mm

Three-act play with epilogue
3幕とエピローグの戯曲

058

Válčení civilistovo / Stanislav Kostka Neumann
Civilian's War / Stanislav Kostka Neumann
市民の戦争 / スタニスラフ・コストカ・ノイマン
1925 / 1st ed. 初版 / 210mm×130mm

War memoirs
戦争の思い出

059

Periferie / František Langer
Periphery / Frantisek Langer
郊外 / フランチシェク・ラングル
1925 / 1st ed. 初版 / 175mm×108mm

19-scene play based on Dostoevsky's 'Crime and Punishment'
ドストエフスキーの「罪と罰」をモチーフとした19場の戯曲

060

V ponorkovém pásmu / Eugène O'Neill
In the Zone / Eugène O'Neill
喫水線で / ユージン・オニール
1925 / 1st ed. 初版 / 190mm×143mm

One-act play
1幕の戯曲

061

O nejbližších věcech / Karel Čapek
Intimate Things / Karel Čapek
最も身近なものについて / カレル・チャペック
1925 / 1st ed. 初版 / 199mm×125mm

Essays

エッセイ

062

O nejbližších věcech / Karel Čapek
Intimate Things / Karel Čapek
最も身近なものについて / カレル・チャペック
1927 / 2nd ed. 2版 / 200mm×125mm

Essays

エッセイ

063

Probuzení / Josef Hora
Awakening / Josef Hora
目覚め / ヨゼフ・ホラ
1925 / 1st ed. 初版 / 200mm×125mm

Fiction

小説

064

Lidumil na kříži / Čestmír Jeřábek
Philanthropist on the Cross / Čestmír Jeřábek
十字架の上の博愛主義者 / チェストミール・イェジャーベック
1925 / 1st ed. 初版 / 192mm×146mm

Detective story
推理小説

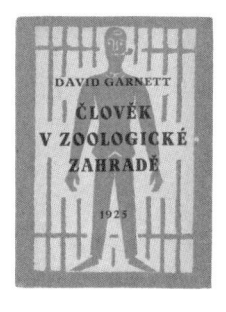

065

Člověk v zoologické zahradě / David Garnett
A Man in the Zoo / David Garnett
動物園の人間 / デビッド・ガーネット
1925 / 1st ed. 初版 / 194mm×144mm

See P94 / P94 参照

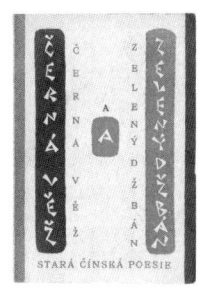

066

Černá věž a zelený džbán
Black Tower and Green Pitcher
黒い塔と緑の水差し
1925 / 1st ed. 初版 / 210mm×145mm

Ancient Chinese poetry,
translated and with an Afterword by B. Mathesius
古い中国の詩　B.マテジウス訳、後書き

067

Života bído, přec tě mám rád / Fráňa Šrámek
Life, You're Penury, But I Still Love You / Fráňa Šrámek
生活の貧困よ、それでも私はおまえが好きだ / フラーニャ・シュラーメック
1924 / 1st ed. 初版 / 196mm×134mm

First poetry collection
初めての詩集

068

Dáma v lišku / David Garnett
Lady into Fox / David Garnett
キツネになった貴婦人 / デビッド・ガーネット
1925 / 1st ed. 初版 / 194mm×146mm

Fiction Translaed by K. Klaus.
Tale of a man horrified to discover his beloved wife has become a fox.

小説　K.クラウス訳
妻になった最愛の女性がキツネになってしまい、恐ろしく思う男の物語。

069

Krakonošova zahrada / Bratří Čapkové
Krakonoš's Garden / Josef & Karel Čapek
クラコノシュの庭 / チャペック兄弟
1926 / 2nd ed. 2版 / 210mm×150mm

Short stories from 1908-11
1908年 - 11年の短編集

070

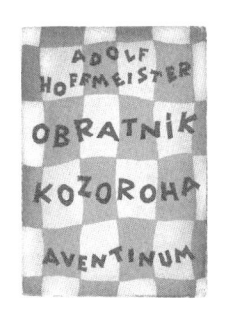

Obratník kozoroha / Adolf Hoffmeister
Tropic of Capricorn / Adolf Hoffmeister
南回帰線 / アドルフ・ホフマイステル
1926 / 1st ed. 初版 / 210mm×148mm

Fiction
小説

071

Kapitol / Harvey Fergusson
Capitol Hill / Harvey Fergusson
連邦議会議事堂 / ハーヴェイ・ファーガソン
1926 / 1st ed. 初版 / 195mm×146mm

Fiction translated by S. V. Klima
小説　S.V.クリーマ訳

072

Města a roky / Konstantin Fedin
Cities and Years / Konstantin Fedin
町と歳月 / コンスタンチン・フェージン
1926 / 1st ed. 初版 / 194mm×145mm

Fiction Translated by B. Muzik.
小説　B.ムジーク訳

073

Hlídač č.47 / Josef Kopta
Watchman No 47 / Josef Kopta
線路番No.47 / ヨゼフ・コプタ
1926 / 1st ed. 初版 / 215mm×138mm

Story of a lonely Czech railwayman.

孤独なチェコの鉄道員の物語

074

Předměstské povídky / František Langer
Stories from the Suburbs / František Langer
郊外の物語 / フランチシェク・ラングル
1926 / 1st ed. 初版 / 192mm×132mm

Short stories

短編集

075

Nebezpečná stáři / Rose Macaulay
Dangerous Ages / Rose Macaulay
危険な老齢 / ローズ・マコーレイ
1926 / 1st ed. 初版 / 200mm×140mm

Fiction Translated by M. Fantová

小説　M.ファントヴァー訳

076

Utrpení pětihranného Boba / Jiří Mařánek
Suffering of Pentagonal Bob / Jiří Mařánek
5角形のボブの受難 / イジー・マジャーネック
1926 / 1st ed. 初版 / 205mm×132mm

077

Utrpení pětihranného Boba / Jiří Mařánek
Suffering of Pentagonal Bob / Jiří Mařánek
5角形のボブの受難 / イジー・マジャーネック
1926 / Hard bound ハードカバー / 205mm×132mm

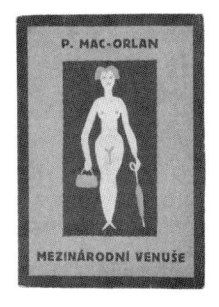

078

Mezinárodní Venuše / Pierre Mac Orlan
La Venus Internationale (International Venus) / Pierre Mac Orlan
国際的なヴィーナス / ピエール・マック・オルラン
1926 / 1st ed. 初版 / 198mm×139mm

Fiction Translated by J. Heyduk
小説　J.ヘイドゥク訳

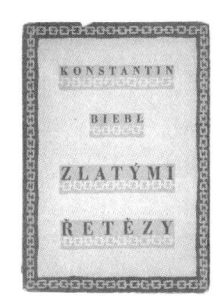

079

Zlatými Řetězy / Konstantin Biebl
With Chains of Gold / Konstantin Biebl
黄金の鎖で / コンスタンチン・ビーブル
1926 / 1st ed. 初版 / 289mm×208mm

Poetry
詩集

080

Jack Spurlock, marnotratný syn / George Horace Lorrimer
Jack Spurlock - Prodigal / George Horace Lorrimer
放蕩息子、ジャック・スパーロック / ジョージ・ホーレス・ロリマー
1926 / 1st ed. 初版 / 196mm×135mm

Fiction Translated by E. Horlivá
小説　E.ホルリヴァー訳

081

Dvojníci a sny / František Kubka
Doppelgängers and Dreams / František Kubka
ドッペルゲンガーと夢 / フランチシェク・クブカ
1926 / 1st ed. 初版 / 210mm×147mm

Fiction
小説

082

Rozmarné léto / Vladislav Vančura
Gay Summer / Vladislav Vančura
陽気な夏 / ヴラジスラフ・ヴァンチュラ
1926 / 1st ed. 初版 / 197mm×135mm

Humorous fiction.
Summer spent by three middle-aged men and a couple of itinerant players

ユーモア小説
3人の中年男と旅芸人の男女の一夏の物語

083

Ráj ve stínu mečů / Henri de Montherlant
Le Paradis A L'ombre Des Epees (Paradise in the Shadow of Swords) / Henri de Montherlant
剣の影の楽園 / アンリ・ド・モンテルラン
1926 / 1st ed. 初版 / 213mm×135mm

Five stories translated by Fr. Sedláček

5つの短編集　Fr. セドラーチェック訳

084

Slova a krev / Giovanni Papini
Words and Blood / Giovanni Papini
言葉と血 / ジョヴァンニ・パピーニ
1926 / 1st ed. 初版 / 212mm×132mm

Short stories translated by J. Skalický

短編集　J. スカリツキー訳

085

Ostrov veliké lásky / Fráňa Šrámek
Island of Great Love / Fráňa Šrámek
大きな愛の島 / フラーニャ・シュラーメック
1926 / 1st ed. 初版 / 210mm×135mm

Three-act comedy

3幕の喜劇

086

Příběhy ryšavého Hanrahana / W. B. Yeats
Stories of Red Hanrahan / W. B. Yeats
赤毛のハンラハン物語 / ウイリアム・バトラー・イェーツ
1926 / 1st ed. 初版 / 217mm×136mm

087

Adam Stvořitel / Bratři Čapkové
Adam the Creator / Josef & Karel Čapek
創造者アダム / チャペック兄弟
1927 / 3rd ed. 3版 / 216mm×135mm

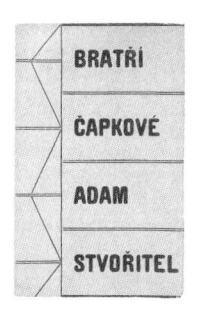

088

Adam Stvořitel / Bratří Čapkové
Adam the Creator / Josef & Karel Čapek
創造者アダム / チャペック兄弟
1928 / 5th ed. 5版 / 213mm×135mm

089

Hry s lidmi i věcmi / Josef Kopta
Game with People and Things / Josef Kopta
人や物との遊び / ヨゼフ・コプタ
1927 / 1st ed. 初版 / 174mm×112mm

090

Grand hotel Nevada / František Langer
Grand Hotel Nevada / František Langer
ネヴァダ・グランドホテル / フランチシェク・ラングル
1927 / 1st ed. 初版 / 213mm×316mm

091

Všechny cesty vedou na Kalvarii / Jerome K. Jerome
All Roads Lead to Calvary / Jerome K. Jerome
すべての道はカルヴァリ (ゴルゴダの丘) に通ず /
ジェローム・クラプカ・ジェローム
1927 / 1st ed. 初版 / 200mm×143mm

092

Putování na dluh / A. C. Nor
Wandering on Credit / A. C. Nor
無銭放浪 / A. C. ノル
1927 / 1st ed. 初版 / 201mm×140mm

Essays on living and travelling rough
放浪と旅のエッセイ

093

Okolo nás / Karel Poláček
Around Us / Karel Poláček
我々の周辺 / カレル・ポラーチェク
1927 / 1st ed. 初版 / 175mm×111mm

Short stories
短編集

094

Přistav mrtvých vod / Pierre Mac Orlan
Port of Dead Water / Pierre Mac Orlan
よどんだ水の港 / ピエール・マッコルラン
1927 / 1st ed. 初版 / 215mm×135mm

095

Diktátor / Jules Romains
Le Dictateur (The Dictator) / Jules Romains
独裁者 / ジュール・ロマン
1927 / 1st ed. 初版 / 215mm×135mm

Four-act play

4幕の戯曲

096

Hvězdy v oknech / Mira Moravec
Stars in the Window / Mira Moravec
窓の中の星 / ミーラ・モラヴェツ
1927 / 1st ed. 初版 / 220mm×150mm

Poetry from 1921-23

1921-23年の詩集

097

Ledacos / Josef Čapek
All Sorts of Things / Josef Čapek
あれやこれや / ヨゼフ・チャペック
1928 / 1st ed. 初版 / 198mm×128mm

Essays

エッセイ

098

Ledacos / Josef Čapek
All Sorts of Things / Josef Čapek
あれやこれや / ヨゼフ・チャペック
1929 / 2nd ed. 2版 / 200mm×123mm

Essays

エッセイ

099

Půlnoční zpověď / Georges Duhamel
Confession de Minuit (Midnight Confession) / Georges Duhamel
深夜の告白 / ジョルジュ・デュアメル
1928 / 1st ed. 初版 / 215mm×135mm

Fiction Translated by J. Hrdinová

小説　J.フルジノヴァー訳

100

Mámení / Helena Dvořáková
Delusions / Helena Dvořáková
妄想 / ヘレナ・ドヴォジャーコヴァー
1928 / 6th ed. 6版 / 190mm×150mm

Fiction

小説

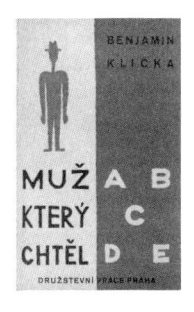

101

Muž který chtěl ABCDE / Benjamin Klička
The Man Who Desired ABCDE / Benjamin Klička
ABCDEを欲しがった男 / ベンジャミン・クリチカ
1928 / 1st ed. 初版 / 204mm×132mm, 198mm×13mm

See P158 / P158 参照

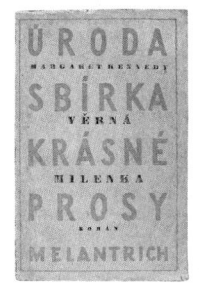

102

Věrná milenka / Margaret Kennedy
The Constant Nymph / Margaret Kennedy
誠実な恋人 / マーガレット・ケネディ
1928 / 1st ed. 初版 / 203mm×130mm

Fiction Translated by L. Baštecká

小説　L.バシュテツカー訳

103

Pestré osmero / Benjamin Klička
Eight Multi-coloured Pieces / Benjamin Klička
色とりどりの8篇 / ベンジャミン・クリチカ
1928 / 1st ed. 初版 / 195mm×125mm

Eight stories

8つの短編

104

Olbřim / Edmond Konrád
Colossus / Edmond Konrád
巨像 / エドモント・コンラート
1928 / 1st ed. 初版 / 215mm×136mm

Play with 9 scenes

9場の戯曲

105

Crewský vlak / Rose Macaulay
Crewe Train / Rose Macaulay
クルーの列車 / ローズ・マコーレイ
1929 / 1st ed. 初版 / 188mm×130mm

Fiction

小説

106

Náměstí republiky / Marie Majerová
Republic Square / Marie Majerová
共和国広場 / マリエ・マイエロヴァー
1929 / 1st ed. 初版 / 193mm×125mm

Fiction

小説

107

Láska není všecko / Olga Scheinpflugová
Love Isn't Everything / Olga Scheinpflugová
愛がすべてではない / オルガ・シャインフルゴヴァー
1929 / 2nd ed. 2版 / 195mm×124mm

Three-act comedy.
Authored by Karel Čapek's wife.

3幕の喜劇
オルガ・シャインフルゴヴァーはカレル・チャペック夫人

108

Žid Süss / Lion Feuchtwanger
Jud Süß (The Jew Süss) / Lion Feuchtwanger
ユダヤ人ジュース / リオン・フォイヒトヴァンガー
1929 / Edition unknown 版不明 / 203mm×137mm

Historical novel on racial problems. Translated by B. Rovensky

人種問題をテーマとした歴史小説　B.ロヴェンスキー訳

109

Pět Hříšníků u velryby / Josef Kopta
Five Sinners by a Whale / Josef Kopta
くじらのもとの5人の罪人 / ヨゼフ・コプタ
1930 / 4th ed. 4版 / 193mm×123mm

Short stories

短編集

110

Bratři Schellenbergové / Bernhard Kellermann
Die Brüder Schellenberg (The Schellenberg Brothers) / Bernhard Kellermann
シェレンベルク兄弟 / ベルンハルト・ケラーマン
1930 / 3rd ed. 3版 / 197mm×124mm

Fiction

小説

111

Továrník Dodsworth / Sinclair Lewis
Dodsworth / Sinclair Lewis
工場主、ドッズワース / シンクレア・ルイス
1931 / 1st ed. 初版 / 225mm×145mm

Translated by E. Horlivá
A retired businessman loses his love and recovers it.

E.ホルリヴァー訳
引退した実業家を主人公としてその愛の破綻と再生を描く

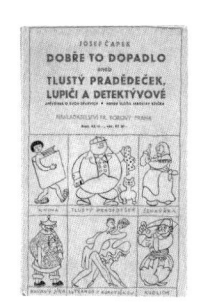

112

Dobře to dopadlo aneb Tlustý pradědeček, lupiči a detektývové / Josef Čapek
'All's Well That Ends Well, Or The Fat Great-Granddad,
the Thief and the Detectives' / Josef Čapek
うまくいった、あるいは太ったひいおじいさんと泥棒と探偵たち / ヨゼフ・チャペック
1932 / 1st ed. 初版 / 198mm×123mm

Two-act play for younger and older children
小さなそして大きな子供たちのための2幕の戯曲

113

Velbloud uchem jehly / František Langer
A Camel through the Eye of a Needle / František Langer
針の目を通ったラクダ / フランチシェク・ラングル
1934 / 1st ed. 初版 / 215mm×138mm

Three-act comedy.
The son of a wealthy family seeks a bride of lowly birth for the sake of
the family's blood.

3幕の喜劇
金持ちの息子が家系の血をさびつかせないようにするために貧しい少女と
結婚しようとする話

114

Kulhavý poutník (Co jsem na světě uviděl) / Josef Čapek
Limping Wanderer (What I Saw in the World) / Josef Čapek
片足をひきずって歩く放浪者(私が世界で何を見たか) / ヨゼフ・チャペック
1937 / 4th ed. 4版 / 198mm×125mm

Philosophical essays. Important work showing Josef's attempts to
understand the meaning and purpose of existence.

哲学的なエッセイで、ヨゼフの著作の中でも
人間が存在する意味や本質を理解しようという努力をしたものとして
重要な作品となっている

115

Továrna na absolutno / Karel Čapek
The Absolute at Large / Karel Čapek
絶対子工場 / カレル・チャペック
1922 / 1st ed. 初版 / 195mm×145mm
1990 / 木魂社

See P178 / P178 参照

116

Kniha lesů, vod a strání / Stanislav Kostka Neumann
The Book of Woodland, Water and Hillsides / Stanislav Kostka Neumann
森と水と山腹の本 / スタニスラフ・コストカ・ノイマン
1938 / 3rd ed. 3版 / 215mm×139mm

Poetry from 1900-13

1900 - 13年の詩集

117

Kořeny / Ladislav Stehlík
Roots / Ladislav Stehlík
根 / ラジスラフ・ステフリーク
1938 / 1st ed. 初版 / 195mm×125mm

Poetry

詩集

118

Zahradníkův rok / Karel Čapek
The Gardener's Year / Karel Čapek
園芸家12カ月 / カレル・チャペック
1947 / Edition unknown 版不明 / 180mm×115mm
1975 / 中央公論社 他

Essays on each month's tasks in the garden
1月から12月まで、月別に園芸家が庭で何をするかをエッセイ風に描いた

119

Bidýlko / Emil Vachek
Perch / Emil Vachek
とまり木 / エミル・ヴァヘック
1954 / 1st edition from Czechoslovakian Writers Press
12版（チェコスロバキア作家出版として初版）/ 215mm×135mm

Story of a good-hearted thief in Prague
スタヴィノハという名のジシュコフ（プラハのある地区）の気のいい泥棒の物語

ヨゼフ・チャペック

1887年3月チェコ・フロノフ生まれ。
『ダーシェンカ あるいは子犬の生活』や
「ロボット」という言葉を世界に広めた戯曲『R.U.R.』
(ロッスムのユニバーサルロボット)で有名なカレル・チャペックの兄。
画家、劇作家、芸術評論家、挿絵画家、舞台芸術家、
書籍のグラフィックアーティストなど、様々な肩書きを持つ。
1910年前後、カレルと共著で評論、散文などを執筆。
以後、1916年にチャペック兄弟としてデビュー。
カレルのほとんどの装丁、挿絵をデザインする。

Josef Čapek

Born in Hronov, Czechoslovakia in March 1887.
Elder brother of Karel Čapek, famous for his plays
"R.U.R." (which brought the word "robot" into the world)
and "Dasenka: The Life of a Puppy (Dasenka cili zivot stenete)".
Josef Čapek's wide range of professional roles included artist,
playwright, art critic, illustrator, cartoonist, stage designer, and book designer.
From1910, he collaborated with Karel
in writing critical essays and prose,
debuting in 1916 as the Čapek Brothers.
Josef designed and illustrated almost all of his brother's books.

※参考資料 / Reference Materials

『Josef Čapek a kniha』
Publishing: Nakladatelství československých výtvarných umělců
Author: Jiří Kotalík - Vladimír Thiele
1959 Praha
Translations: from P19 to P20 (4 lines from the bottom)
『O sobě』
Publishing: Československý spisovatel
Author: Josef Čapek
1958 Praha
Translations: from P85 - P87, P88 - P90 (15 lines from the above)

※イラスト / Illustrations

All illustrations by Josef Čapek.
『Josef Čapek a kniha』
Publishing: Nakladatelství československých výtvarných umělců
Author: Jiří Kotalík - Vladimír Thiele
1959 Praha

チャペックの本棚 ｜ ヨゼフ・チャペックの装丁デザイン

訳者
千野栄一
千野亜矢子
スー・ハーバート
エヴァ・フソヴァー
パメラ・ミキ

ブックデザイン
出原速夫

協力
ヤロスラヴ・ドスタール
フランチシェック・ドスタール
カテジナ・ドスターロヴァー

スペシャルサンクス
ハナ・ワーグネロヴァー
鈴木裕子
安達万里子 (まめ工房)
加藤希

タイトル
小澤研太郎

編集
及川さえ子

発行人
三芳伸吾

Čapek's Bookshelf | The Book Design of Josef Čapek

Translated by :
Eiichi Chino
Ayako Chino
Sue Herbert
Eva Husová
Pamela Miki

Book Design :
Hayao Izuhara

Cooperated by :
MUDr. Jaroslav Dostál
František Dostál
Kateřina Dostálová

Special thanks :
Hana Wagnerová
Hiroko Suzuki
Mariko Adachi (Mame Koubou)
Nozomi Kato

Title :
Kentaro Ozawa

Editor :
Saeco Oikawa

Publisher :
Shingo Miyoshi

チャペックの本棚｜ヨゼフ・チャペックの装丁デザイン
Čapek's Bookshelf | The Book Design of Josef Čapek

2003年3月12日初版第1刷発行

編集
及川さえ子
発行人
三芳伸吾
発行所
ピエ・ブックス

〒170-0003 東京都豊島区駒込4-14-6-301
編集　TEL: 03-3949-5010　FAX: 03-3949-5650
editor@piebooks.com
営業　TEL: 03-3940-8302　FAX: 03-3576-7361
sales@piebooks.com
http://www.piebooks.com

P・I・E BOOKS
Villa Phoenix Suite 301, 4-14-6, Komagome, Toshima-ku,
Tokyo 170-0003 Japan
TEL: +81-3-3940-8302　FAX: +81-3-3576-7361

印刷・製本　株式会社東京印書館
プリンティングディレクター　高柳昇

Copyright © 2003 PIE BOOKS
Printed in Japan
ISBN4-89444-249-3　C0070

本書の収録内容の無断転載、複写、引用等を禁じます。
ご注文、乱丁、落丁本の交換などに関するお問い合わせは、
小社営業部までご連絡ください。

2003年3月17日から住所・電話・FAX番号が変わります。
〒170-0005 東京都豊島区南大塚2-32-4
編集 Tel: 03-5395-4820　Fax: 03-5395-4821
営業 Tel: 03-5395-4811　Fax: 03-5395-4812

Please note our change of contact details from 17th March 2003.
2-32-4, Minami-Otsuka, Toshima-ku, Tokyo 170-0005 Japan
TEL: +81-3-5395-4811　FAX: +81-3-5395-4812